MEDIUM ÆVUM M(

NEW SERIES ..

A DESCRIPTIVE INDEX OF

THE ENGLISH LYRICS IN

JOHN OF GRIMESTONE'S PREACHING BOOK

By

EDWARD WILSON

THE SOCIETY FOR THE STUDY OF
MEDIEVAL LANGUAGES AND LITERATURE

http://mediumaevum.modhist.ox.ac.uk

ISBN-13: 978-0-907570-68-4 (pb)

This digital reprint first issued 2015

i

PREFACE

H.G. Pfander long ago drew attention to the alphabetical reference books of the Friars (see Medium AEvum III (1934)), and selections from the alphabetical preaching book of John of Grimestone (MS. Advocates' Library 18.7.21. in the National Library of Scotland) have appeared in journals and anthologies (notably Carleton Brown's Religious Lyrics of the XIVth Century which was first published in 1924). Most recently, further unpublished items have been printed in Miss Woolf's The English Religious Lyric in the Middle Ages (1968).

This volume is intended to make accessible the manuscript's collection of English lyrics as a whole, and to this end I have borrowed the notion of a 'Descriptive Index' from Dr. A.G. Rigg's A Glastonbury Miscellany (1968), though on a more restricted scale. There are listed here 246 items, of which 182 have been hitherto unprinted from this manuscript (10 of the 182 exist in other manu- scripts and some of these versions have been printed elsewhere), and 108 items are unrecorded in The Index of Middle English Verse and its Supplement.

If many of the texts are the daisies and dandelions of fourteenth century poetry, then they are best seen in a mass. These are the lyrics and tags which a Norfolk Franciscan assembled in 1372, and it is this preciseness in localization of date, place, and intellectual background which makes Grimestone's collection so valuable.

I am grateful to the Trustees of the National Library of Scotland for per- mission to publish material from MS. Advocates' Library 18.7.21. I should also like to thank Dr. A.B. Emden who supplied me with a reference to a John of

Grimestone and gave much help with the biographical problems; Dr. N.R. Ker

who gave great aid in palaeographical matters (including a number of readings);

Professor P.G. Walsh who gave much help with the Latin transcriptions; and

Professor A. McIntosh who made a graphemic analysis of the manuscript and dis-

cussed many particular textual problems with me.

Publication of this monograph has been made possible by generous sub-

ventions from the Carnegie Trust for the Universities of Scotland and from the

University of Edinburgh.

iii

CONTENTS

Abbreviations

AH	Analecta Hymnica ed. G.M. Dreves and C. Blume (Leipzig 1886–1922)
Bennett and Smithers	J.A.W. Bennett and G.V. Smithers (with Glossary by N. Davis) Early Middle English Verse and Prose (2nd ed. Oxford 1968)
DOST	Dictionary of the Older Scottish Tongue
EETS OS	Early English Text Society Original Series
EL XIII	Carleton Brown English Lyrics of the XIIIth Century (Oxford 1932)
Index	C. Brown and R.H. Robbins The Index of Middle English Verse (New York 1943)
Initia	H. Walther Initia carminum ac versuum medii aevi posterioris latinorum (2nd ed. Göttingen 1969)
JEGP	Journal of English and Germanic Philology
MED	Middle English Dictionary
MLN	Modern Language Notes
MP	Modern Philology
Obertello	A. Obertello Liriche Religiose Inglesi del Secolo Quattordicesimo (Milan 1947)
OED	Oxford English Dictionary
PL	Patrologia Latina
RL XIV	C. Brown Religious Lyrics of the XIVth Century (2nd ed. rev. by G.V. Smithers Oxford 1957)

RL XV   C. Brown Religious Lyrics of the XVth Century

(Oxford 1939)

Sprichw.   H. Walther Proverbia sententiaeque latinitatis medii

aevi 6 vols. (Göttingen 1963-9)

Suppl.   R.H. Robbins and J.L. Cutler Supplement to the Index

of Middle English Verse (Lexington 1965)

Whiting   B.J. Whiting and H.W. Whiting Proverbs, Sentences,

and Proverbial Phrases from English Writings Mainly

before 1500 (Cambridge, Mass. and London 1968)

Woolf   R. Woolf The English Religious Lyric in the Middle Ages

(Oxford 1968)

Description of the Manuscript

iii (i and ii modern) + 166 + ii (both modern); parchment (flyleaves all paper;

flyleaf iii at the front has half a watermark, unidentifiable); 6.9 x 4.7 inches;

the notes are on 31 ruled long lines per page within a ruled frame (5.7 x 3.7

inches); modern foliation in pencil; modern binding (rebound 24 April 1931);

secundo folio (of the introductory leaves) luste saluari.

The manuscript is probably incomplete: the last three headings in the Index

to the preaching notes (De Vsura, De Vita, De Veste) are missing from the text

at the end.

There is only one catchword or signature visible (f. 58^v); others may have

been lost through shaved margins (there may be the top of one at f. 46^v). It has

not proved possible to give a certain collation.

Although Dr. R.H. Robbins has spoken of two hands (JEGP XXXIX (1940)

234), Dr. N.R. Ker has informed me that he thinks that the preliminary leaves,

the notes, and all the English and Latin verses are in one hand. There is a

facsimile of f. 6 facing p. 118 of Obertello.

Contents

The reference is to be found in <u>Clementinarum</u> Liber III

titulus vii, cap. ii, ed. Æ. Friedberg <u>Corpus</u> <u>Iuris</u>

<u>Canonici</u>, <u>Pars</u> <u>Secunda</u>: <u>Decretalium</u> <u>Collectiones</u> (Leipzig

1881) col. 1161-4. According to A.G. Little <u>Franciscan</u>

<u>Papers</u>, <u>Lists</u>, <u>and</u> <u>Documents</u> (Manchester 1943) p. 241

Clement V's Decretals reached England early in 1318.

MS.: Patet.

10^{v} [(a) Latin verses on the 15 days before Doomsday, etc.; not in

<u>Initia</u> or <u>Sprichw.</u>]

[b] Vas condimenti preponi debe[t] edenti,

Nam sapit esca male, que datur ab[s] que sale.

<u>Initia</u> 20042, <u>Sprichw.</u> 32908. MS.: debēt; abque.

[c] Quis fuit mortuus et non natus?   Adam.

Quis fuit natus et non mortuus? Helias et Enoc

Six such questions in all.

[(d) Lyric no. 10]

11-166^{v} [Preaching notes, with lyrics 11-246]

The Preaching Notes

The preaching notes, mainly in Latin, consist of quotations and what the manuscript's Index to the notes describes as narraciones bonas and multas notabilitates in Anglico (f. 9^v), grouped under headings from De Abstinencia to De Via Christi (the manuscript Index's last three topics are missing from the text; see the description of the manuscript). The only French items which I have noted are on ff. 27^v, 46, 110, and 126.

Besides the numerous quotations from the Bible, references are especially frequent to Cicero, Seneca, Ambrose, Chrysostom, Gregory the Great, Anselm, Bernard of Clairvaux, Hugh and Richard of St. Victor, Isidore, and the Glossa Ordinaria. Other authorities include: Aristotle's Ethics (f. 69), Valerius Maximus, the Gospel of Nicodemus (f. 136), Origen, Cyprian, Eusebius, Macrobius (ff. 55^v, 69), Boethius (ff. 36^v and 112^v), Cassiodorus, Bede, Rabanus Maurus, Peter Damian (f. 107^v), Peter Comestor (f. 47), John Beleth (f. 55^v), Grosseteste (f. 20^v), Aquinas, and Durandus' Summa Theologica (f. 70).*

The prologue to Lyric 232, with its reference to Remigius of Auxerre, the verb depingitur, and the mottoes, is clearly a sermon 'picture' of the kind which Miss Smalley has shown us in her 'classicising' friars, notably John Ridevall and Robert Holcot.[1] But other references to Remigius (ff. 27^v, 42^v, 68^v, 75^v, and 159^v) and to 'Holkote' (f. 54) have no such pictures.

* The folio references in this section do not pretend to be exhaustive.

Some evidence of the revival of interest in the thirteenth century Franciscan

Thomas de Docking is seen in the citation Nota secundum Dockingge in postilla

sua (f. 58).[2]

That this is a Franciscan compilation can be seen from a number of

references. A whole section (ff. 137-9^v) is headed De Regula Beati Francisci;

it begins:

Nota quod Beatus Franciscus fecit tres regulas: scilicet, illam

quam confirmauit sibi Papa Innocencius sine bulla; postea fecit

aliam breuiorem et hec perdita fuit; postea illam eamdem quam

Papa Honorius confirmauit cum bulla. De qua regula multa fuerunt

extracta per ministros contra voluntatem Beati Francisci.

Postquam secunda regula quam fecit ...

Unidentified in the manuscript, this is chapter i of the Speculum Perfectionis

compiled in 1318.[3] The text of the Regula bullata of 1223 is given on

ff. 137^v-9^v.[4]

Elsewhere, there are three quotations from the Actus Beati Francisci et

Sociorum Ejus:[5]

(i)   s.v. De Obediencia, ff. 96^v-97: chap. ii, Sabatier pp. 8-11;

(ii)   s.v. De Ocupacione, ff. 97^v-98: chap. viii, Sabatier pp. 27-30;

(iii) s.v. De Paciencia, ff. 110^v-11: chap. iv.4-the end, Sabatier

      pp. 17-19.

Provenance, Date, and Language

There are the following indications of provenance and date:

I.   Orate pro anima fratris Iohannis de Grimistone qui scripsit

istum librum cum magna solicitudine Anno domini 1372 Aue

maria pro anima sua pro amore dei   (f. 9^v)

Thus John of Grimestone was a friar, and from the Franciscan content of

some entries (see above, 'The Preaching Notes') he must have been a Franciscan

friar.   There are four references known to a fourteenth century Franciscan John

of Grimestone:

(i), (ii)   In the Register of Divers Letters of Roger Martival, Bishop

of Salisbury, in two lists of Friars Minors licensed to hear

confessions appear (a) 'fratrem Johannem de Grymston' ...

ordinis Minorum Dorc'' (15 March 1327); (b) 'Johannes de

Grimston'' (21 March 1329). [11]

(iii)   In the Register of Ralph of Shrewsbury, Bishop of Bath and

Wells, is a licence, dated 10 June 1338, for 'brother John

de Grymston, of the order of Friars Minors, of the convent

of Dorchester, to preach, hear confessions, impose penance

and absolve.' [12]

(iv)   In the Ely Diocesan Records, in a list of 'Minores' licensed

to hear confessions and 'admissi apud Dounham', dated 25

December 1338, is a 'frater Johannes de Grymeston'.

Dr. A.B. Emden has told me that for a friar to be presented for a licence

to hear confessions he should be of mature years, say thirty years of age.   Thus

if the first reference in 1327 is to the Grimestone of the manuscript he would be

about seventy-five in 1372.

Carleton Brown inclined towards the idea that Grimestone was a Yorkshire-
man,[14] but the language, which is that of south-west Norfolk (see below), and
the East Anglian suggestions of III, IV, and V below, would support Professor
Ekwall's suggestion that 'John Grimestone may well have taken his name from
Grimston near King's Lynn (Norfolk)'.[15]

II.   Iste liber est Fratris Nic' [or N] de Roma de dono Fratris Ioh' de

             Grimestone   Aue Maria pro anima sua (f. 9^v)

This inscription, which appears above Grimestone's, is almost completely
erased.   A Nicholas de Rome was a King's scholar at Cambridge in December
1319,[16] although this seems rather early to be the manuscript's man.

III.   Nota de Rob' coldone In ecclesia sancti Nic' Gipis' (right-hand

             margin of f. 60^v in Grimestone's hand in Dr. N.R. Ker's view)

Robert Coldon has not been identified.   The reference to St. Nicholas's
church, Ipswich, suggests that Coldon may be from the place-name found in
fourteenth century Suffolk documents,[17] although Coldon was also a Yorkshire
place-name (modern Cowden, East Riding).

IV.   Th' Chantebi (left-hand margin of f. 60^v; same hand as III)

In view of III above and V below, it is tempting to think that this must be
the same man as Thomas Chauntbien who was at St. Nicholas's church, Ipswich,
in 1327.[18]

V.   On f. 87, s.v. De Morte, is the story 'De duobus tabernariis apud

             Gip'' (i.e. Ipswich) who ate and drank well and said 'fy de morte';

             in the morning they could scarcely be buried for the stench (of their bodies).

It looks as though the story may have been included for its local interest.

There are the following indications of later provenance:

A.   Two entries, possibly in the same hand of c. 1500:

(i)   Memorandum that ser thomas helder howyt to me [?] cornell

for a bow that y scollt to hym   xxd

Item to ser water hankke [or haukke] for a choppe [?] clott

prys the yard   xxxs and [...?] (f. 67^V)

None of the three names has been identified; the use of ser presumably

indicates that Helder and Hankke were priests.

(ii)   that I haw ou [?] the abbot of sent tomas cort

for v pont of sufyr [?]   xxid (f. 156^V)

The reference has not been identified.

B.   Iste liber constat wililmo broin quem deus amat et deabolus

odit (f. 108^V)

This hand is also c. 1500 in date; Broin has not been identified.

C.   Ex Libris Jacobis Stuart 1699 (f. 67^V)

This inscription occurs twice, and both times the name (visible under

ultra-violet light) has been erased. Stuart has not been identified.

D.   Guililmus Young 1702 (flyleaf iii)

Young, whose surname also appears on f.3, has not been identified.

It is not known when the manuscript was acquired by the Advocates'

Library, but Mr. I.C. Cunningham of the National Library of Scotland has told

me that it first appears in an unprinted Advocates' Library catalogue of c. 1825
(F.R. 216), and that it was probably acquired in the quarter century preceding
that, as it does not appear in any of the eighteenth century catalogues.

The language of the lyrics was described by Carleton Brown as 'that of the
northern border of the East Midlands.   On the basis of the linguistic forms we
may take the Humber as the northern and Norfolk as the southern limit for these
poems'.[19]   Professor R.L. Greene similarly called the language 'that of the
northern part of the East Midland region'.[20]   However, the view of Professor
Ekwall, that the dialect was 'probably a Norfolk one',[21] is confirmed by the
graphemic analysis which Professor McIntosh has made of this transcript.   His
conclusion, based on 268 test questions, is that the manuscript belongs to south-
west Norfolk.[22]

Notes

1. See B. Smalley, English Friars and Antiquity in the Early Fourteenth Century
   (Oxford 1960) pp. 112ff., 165ff.

2. On Thomas de Docking see J.I. Catto, 'New Light on Thomas Docking
   O.F.M.', Mediaeval and Renaissance Studies VI (1968) 135-49.

3. ed. P. Sabatier, British Society of Franciscan Studies XIII (Manchester
   1928) pp. xxii-xxv, 1-3; the notes are in BSFS XVII (Manchester 1931).

4. For a text, see Opuscula Sancti Patris Francisci Assiensis (3rd ed.
   Quarracchi 1949) I 63-74.

5. ed. P. Sabatier, Collection D'Etudes et de Documents Sur L'Histoire
   Religieuse et Littéraire du Moyen Age IV (Paris 1902). There are some
   considerable divergences from Sabatier's text. In some but by no means
   all instances Grimestone's version agrees with one in section ii (ff.
   65^v-104) of Dr. A.G. Little's manuscript, described by him in Collectanea
   Franciscana I ed. A.G. Little et al. BSFS V (Aberdeen 1914), where see
   pp. 48, 50, and 49 for the parallels. This manuscript is now Bodleian MS.
   Lat.th.d.23, and is described by R.B. Brooke in her edition of Scripta
   Leonis ... (Oxford 1970) pp. 37-39.

6. The list is necessarily imprecise as it includes the manuscript's attributions
   to more general sources (e.g. no. 34), but the numbers, if approximate,
   are not misleading.
   On this manuscript see J.A. Herbert, Catalogue of Romances in the
   Department of Manuscripts in the British Museum (London 1910) III 166-79.

English lyrics from it were printed by F. J. Furnivall, Political, Religious, and Love Poems EETS OS 15 (2nd ed. 1903) pp. 249-70.

8. On this manuscript see M.R. James, A Descriptive Catalogue of the Manuscripts in the Library of Jesus College, Cambridge (London 1895) pp. 11-12.

9. On this manuscript see H.O. Coxe, Catalogus Codicum Mss. qui in Collegiis Aulisque Oxoniensibus (Oxford 1852) I.

10. On this manuscript see A.T. Bannister, A Descriptive Catalogue of the Manuscripts in the Hereford Cathedral Library (Hereford 1927) pp. 48-49.

11. The Registers of Roger Martival, Bishop of Salisbury 1315-1330 II (bis) The Register of Divers Letters (second half), ed. C.R. Elrington, Canterbury and York Society LVIII (1972) 506 and 601. I owe reference to Martival's Register to Dr. A.B. Emden. Despite the Dorchester (Dorset) reference here and in Ralph of Shrewsbury's Register, the dialect of the preaching book probably rules out as John's home town all Grimstons (including the Dorset one) outside Norfolk and Suffolk (cf. Ely reference and see further below).

12. Quoted from T.S. Holmes, 'The Register of Ralph of Shrewsbury, Bishop of Bath and Wells, 1329-1363' Somerset Record Society IX (1896) 322. It was cited by H.G. Pfander, The Popular Sermon of the Medieval Friar in England (New York 1937) p. 5.

13. Ely Diocesan Records G 1/1, f. 95; the records are now deposited in the University Library, Cambridge. I am grateful to Mrs. A.E.B. Owen for sending me a transcript of the entry, and for the information that Dounham is Downham in the Isle of Ely where the bishop often resided. I owe knowledge of this reference to Grimestone to its citation (from a later

transcript) in a list of friars licensed to preach and hear confessions

during the fourteenth century in J.L. Copeland 'The relations between the

secular clergy and the Mendicant Friars in England during the century after

the issue of the bull Super cathedram (1300)', London M.A. thesis (1938),

p. 58, where the reference in Ralph of Shrewsbury's Register is also noted.

14. RL XIV, pp. xvii-xviii.

15. English Studies XVIII (1936) 225 in a review of Supplements to J.E. Wells's
Manual.

16. A.B. Emden, A Biographical Register of the University of Cambridge to
1500 (Cambridge 1963).

17. E.g.: '... on the high road to Coldone, in the parish of St. Peter, Ipswich',
Catalogue of Ancient Deeds (London 1900) III 4, no. A.3863 (6 Edward III).
For other examples see 'A Descriptive Catalogue of Ancient Deeds in the
Public Record Office', Proceedings of the Suffolk Institute of Archaeology
and Natural History X (1900) pp. 265, no. A.3290 (6 Edw. III); 294,
no. A.3521 (3 Edw. III); 323, no. A.3760 (4 Edw. III).

18. See C. Morley, 'Catalogue of Beneficed Clergy of Suffolk, 1086-1550',
Proceedings of the Suffolk Institute ... XXII (1934-6) 43.

19. RL XIV, pp. xviii-xix.

20. The Early English Carols (Oxford 1935) p. 346.

21. review cited in n.15 above.

22. The questions and the supporting evidence are as yet unpublished.
However, it may be noted that the following spellings were amongst those
used: et = 'it' (5/48); elde (adj.) = 'old' (7/16); michil = 'much' (5/29);

manie = 'many' (14/2); oni = 'any' (87/4); wil = 'while' (68/1; quil also

occurs, 97/1); þoru = 'through' (118/3); hatȝ = 'hath' (24/1); sal = 'shall'

(194/8; xal never occurs); deyȝe (vb.) = 'die' (121/2); thing = 'think'

(199/27); herde = 'earth' (130/1); det = 'death' (185/20). Further

discussion of the linguistic provenance will appear elsewhere.

Notes on the Descriptive Index

The order of presentation is: the subject-heading a lyric appears under,

the folio number, any introductory sentences in the manuscript necessary for

comprehension of the lyric (as in no. 112), and, where the lyric has been printed

before from this manuscript, the opening line(s) (if this is a couplet printed in

Index or Suppl. this is indicated by 'Couplet' prior to the Index/Suppl. number,

as in no.11). If a lyric has been hitherto unprinted from this manuscript, the

full text is given.

Immediately below the English text is printed any Latin source or version

in the manuscript; the source is not necessarily in this position in the manuscript.

Frequently only the opening of the source is printed. To have given the com-

plete text of all the Latin poems would have been to swell the Index unjustifiably,

but where the full text is needed for comprehension of the English it has been

given. If the full text of a poem is not given, the quotation lacks final

punctuation; incomplete prose quotations end: ...

The notes to the poems are mainly bibliographical, in keeping with the

notion of a Descriptive Index. Any Index and Suppl. number is given; its

absence indicates the text is not recorded there. Following any such number,

reference is made to any printed text from the manuscript. Where there is more

than one edition of a lyric, reference where possible has been made to the

anthologies of Carleton Brown (EL XIII, RL XIV, and RL XV); only one edition

is listed (others are given in Index and Suppl.). Substantive errors in the

printed texts are corrected; orthographic ones are not.

Where possible, sources are then identified; except for biblical references

the manuscript's identification of the source of a lyric does not go beyond the

name of the author.   Any Initia and Sprichw. number is given; their absence

indicates that the text is not recorded there.   Verbal variations from the Initia/

Sprichw. texts are not listed.   Items in Whiting are also noted.

The scale of this Index has reduced the extent of the glossing, which is

restricted to words which might give trouble even with the aid of dictionaries

or to words which the unwary might not look up.

The Text

Manuscript abbreviations are silently expanded; punctuation and word-

division are modernized.   Editorial matter is in square brackets; [...] indicates

words lost through damage to the manuscript or through shaved margins; scribal

interlineations are printed within the marks ˋ ʹ. It has not proved possible to use

italic script for Latin, and the alternative frequent underlining would be un-

attractive.

Ampersand is always printed as and to distinguish its use from an which is

the only written-out form; w^t is transcribed with in all cases (e.g. in with

itself, in nouns as withnesse for w^{t}nesse, and in verbs as sewith for sew^t); the

occasional final otiose -is/-es abbreviation (as in spekt, no. 15) has been ignored,

but otherwise this mark is transcribed -is.

Note

    To the anthologies with texts from Grimestone's manuscript which are listed in Index and Suppl. the following may be added (the anthology number is followed in brackets by the Descriptive Index number):

    (i)   Obertello: 9 (5), 10 (8), 11 (180), 12 (213 and 215), 13 (34), 14 (178), p. 228 in notes to 16 (154), 24 (205), 26 (211), 29 (177), 30 (184), 31 (186), 32 (202), 33 (214), 42 (107), 44 (203).

    (ii)   C. and K. Sisam, The Oxford Book of Medieval English Verse (Oxford 1970): 84 (184), 85 (201).

    (iii)   T. Silverstein, Medieval English Lyrics (London 1971): 41 (7), 42 (201), 43 (203), 44 (211).

    D. Gray, Themes and Images in the Medieval English Religious Lyric (London, 1972), appeared too late to incorporate reference to it in the body of the Descriptive Index. Mr. Gray prints thirteen lyrics by Grimestone for the first time (the Gray page number is followed in brackets by the Descriptive Index number): 39 (167), 40 (191), 100 (33), 107 (166), 123 (51), 125 (168, 162), 139 (164), 140-1 (204), 167-8 (52), 268 n.15 (163), 274 n.72 (195), 280 n.32 (210).

1

THE DESCRIPTIVE INDEX

1. f. 1   I wil [...]
            And þus I haue [...]
            Be my feit it [...]
            For woso doth [...]
            Suich smert w[...]
            I wil be war o[...]
            And lafe wordes g[...]
            And sauen boþen fr[...]

    Ms. damaged.

2. f. 1   For þing þat is to askyn
            With stedefast herte and lesten[...]
            With loue and with charite
            With lounesse of herte hou so it [...]
            With good hope of spedingge
            In time þat is nouth to chaleng[...]
            And þat man prey for himself ouer aler.
            Pro debita circum[...]

    Ms. damaged.

3. f. 2   Tel nouth þin frend al þat [...]
            For perauenture or it cum to e[...]
            Sum time þu wenis to ha[...]
            Of wam þat afterward wil[...]
            þerfore boþen nith a[...]
            Beþenk þe wel to wom [...]
            þat þu ne þornouth se[þ or y follows]
            Queþer þu gost or wakst[...]

    Index 3264. Ms. damaged. þornouth: ? = þorn nouth, 'lack not' (OED
    Tharn, v.). Cf. Whiting, F635.

4. f. 2ᵛ   At þe time of matines, Lord, þu were itake
    Index and Suppl. 441. RL XIV, 55. A version of the hymn 'Patris
    sapientia Veritas', AH XXX, 13; see Woolf, pp. 235-6.

5. f. 3^{v} Als I lay vpon a nith
Alone in my longging

Index and Suppl. 352. RL XIV, 56. Speakers indicated in margins: iesu (ll. 9, 129), Christus loquitur (l. 61), iesus (l. 109), and Maria (ll. 21, 105, 125).

6. f. 4^{v} In Bedlem is a child iborn

Index 1472. RL XIV, 57.

7. f. 5^{v} Als I lay vpon a nith
I lokede vpon a stronde

Index and Suppl. 353. RL XIV, 58.

8. f. 6 Lullay, lullay, litel child,
þu þat were so sterne and wild

Index and Suppl. 2024. RL XIV, 59. Facsimile in Obertello, facing p. 118. Spoken not by the Virgin but by a meditator; cf. no. 180.

9. f. 10 Nu is vp, nou is doun;
Nou is frend fo.
Nou is out, nou is nout;
Nou is al ago.

Index and Suppl. 2341. F.A. Patterson's transcript, JEGP XX (1921) 274-5 is inaccurate. Whiting, N179.

10. f. 10^{v} Wat is more dred
And wat is more fled
þan pouerte and penance?
Wat is more knowen
And wat is more blowen
þan bost and bobaunce?

Wat ~~is~~ more conseyled
And wat is more red
þan coueytise and treccherie?
Wat is more vsed
And wat is more spred
þan is lust and lecherie?

Index 3908. conseyled: = 'counselled'.

De Abstinencia

11. f. 12 Alle þe wordis þat drawen to senne
Omne seminarium voluptatis venenum puta.

Couplet. Suppl. 222.5. Attributed in the ms. to Augustine.

ibid.

12. f. 12 þe wise herte and vnderstondingge
Sal kepen himselue fro senningge.
Cor sapiens et intelligibile abstinebit se a peccatis.

Index 3500 (both the previous and the next couplet were included under this number). Ecclesiasticus iii 32.

ibid.

13. f. 12 þanne is abstinence of worþinesse
Tunc est preclara apud Deum abstinencia ...

Couplet. Suppl. 3516.5. Attributed in the ms. to Jerome.

De Adulacione

14. f. 13 þei ben nouth wel for to leuen
þat with manie wordis wil quemen;
For often deceyued þe briddes be
With sundri songes an loueli gle.
Non bene creduntur, nimium qui blanda locuntur

Sprichw. 17281. English and Latin repeated at f. 46^v, s.v. 'De Decepcione', no. 61.

ibid.

15. f. 13 Late lef him þat michil spekt
Raro credatur cuiquam, si multa loquatur

Couplet. Index 1864. Sprichw. 26292. English and Latin repeated at f. 46^v, s.v. 'De Decepcione', no. 62.

ibid.

16. f. 13 ȝef þu ᵕwilt´ ben riche or cleped holi,
Ler to flateren, for þei ben laten wel bi.
Si vis ditari vel ut propheta vocari

Sprichw. 29379. laten wel bi: = 'thought well of' (Latin cari; OED s.v. Let, v.[1], 16).

4

De Auaricia

17.   f. 14   Pecunia maket wrong rith

Suppl. 2743.5.   G.R. Owst Literature and Pulpit in Medieval England
(2nd ed. Oxford 1961) p. 317. Whiting, M630.

ibid.

18.   f. 15   þe þing þat þu mauth ˈlesenˊ, clep et nouth þin owen.

Lift vpward þin herte heuene for to knowen.

þat þe werd þe lenit, he robet it aȝen;

þo þat þe werd despiset, blissed sulen þei ben.

Nil tuum dixeris quod potes perdere

Index 3485.

ibid.

19   f. 15   Werdis blisse maket me blind   Respice

þat of my det I make no mynd.   Ante te

þis werdis welthe is but a gile,

But man be war -- it wil him file.   Retro te

þis werdis blisse is but a wynd

þat blowith abouten to al mankynd.   A dextris

þis werdis blisse is nouth trewe

For after liking it maket to rewe.   Et a sinistris

Index 4222.   Whiting, W671 (this ex. not noted); cf. here nos. 83,
103, and 237.

De Accidia

20.   f. 16   Consilium Diaboli

To pleyȝen and ragen is for þi pru.

Wanne suldest þu pleyȝen betre þan nou?

Wan þu for helde of pley salt blinne,

þanne saltu amenden þe of þi senne.

An doute þe nouth to sennen mikil

For Godes merci was neuere fikil.

Index 3764.   for helde: = 'on account of age (eld)'.

ibid.

21. f. 16   Þe slauwe man is but a driȝe tre þat no froit wil beren.

           Of al is time in þis werld at þe Dom he sal ansueren,

           And afterward han helle pine but penance mou him weren.

Index 3464.   a driȝe tre] tre a driȝe (marked for transposition) MS.

ibid.

22. f. 16   Ȝef þu ȝeuest him eten inou, þanne must him slepen.   homo est of

           Ȝef þu ȝeuest him hunger, þanne wil he wepen.   pore tilþe

           Ȝef þu ȝeuest him richesse, þanne wil he rote;   ideo of

           And ȝef þu ȝef him pouerte, þan can he don no note.   pore tilþe

Index 1431.

De Amore Dei

23. f. 17ᵛ   I ne wot quat is loue

           Nescio quid sit amor

Index and Suppl. 1337.   Owst Literature and Pulpit p. 21 (þouth not youth,
I. 4; n.b. Latin vritur igne graui).   The two English stanzas are
accompanied by Initia 11740, Sprichw. 16531, and Initia 11741, Sprichw.
16532.

ibid.

24. f. 18ᵛ   On þe tre he hatȝ iborn

           Oure sennes for wiche we weren forlorn.

ibid.

25. f. 19   Loue made Crist in Oure Lady to lith

       Index 2011.   RL XIV, p. 266.   Cf. the lyric on f. 119, s.v. 'De Passione
Christi', no. 167.

De Amicicie Dei

26. f. 19   Prelati ecclesie mortui debent esse mundo, non timentes

           propter iusticiam etc. Set:

           Frenchipe is felounie;

           Manchipe is vileynie;

           Clergie is tresorie;

           And borwing is roberie.

Index 873.

6

De Amore Proximi

27. f. 19^V Loke þat þu for no frend be
               Fo to him þat louet þe.
               Noli esse pro amico inimicus proximo tuo.

Index and Suppl. 1942 (listed only at f. 21 where the English and the
Latin are repeated s.v. 'De Amore Inimicorum', no. 30; the item
consists of one couplet and not two as stated by Index and as printed
by Patterson JEGP XX (1921) 275 who includes no. 31).   Ecclesiasticus
vi l.

ibid.

28. f. 19^V He þat louet his frend and fo,
               His loue ne werchet him no wo.
               Dileccio proximi malum non operatur.

Romans xiii 10.   English and Latin repeated at f. 47, s.v. 'De
Dileccione', no. 64.

ibid.

29. f. 20   Loue is blisse in mannis mynde
     Index 2006.   EL XIII, p. 209.

De Amore Inimicorum

30. f. 21   Loke þat þu for no frend be
     See above, f. 19^V, no. 27.

ibid.

31. f. 21   ȝef þu wilt don Godes lore,
               ȝeld harm for harm neueremore.
               Nulli malum pro malo reddentes.
     See above, f. 19^V, no. 27.   Romans xii 17.

De Auro

32. f. 23^V Sic in anima debet esse:
               Clernesse of vnderstondingge;
               Richesse of grace þat is folwingge;
               Clennesse withouten sinningge;
               Hardnesse withouten feinȝengge;
               Buxumnesse withouten grochingge;
               Worþinesse of good doyngge;

Heuinesse of stedefast liuingge.

Claritas sapiencie

Index 634. The Christian soul is likened to the qualities of gold.

De Beata Virgine

33.   f. 23^v Heil Marie, an wel þe be.

Of loue gunne þu lere

Wan Gabriel so grette þe

An rounnede in þin eere.

In blisful time were þu born;

Oure Saueour þu bere.

Al þis werd it were forlorn,

Ne were þat þu ne were.

Suete maiden Marie,

þy [?] rewe nou on me.

Index 1061.   þy: almost certainly not þu (cf. Bennett and Smithers,
8D.7, 24, L. 13, 32) but any descender is lost through a shaved tail
margin (little text can be lost); with this formula cf. RL XIV, 65.25,
124.25, and no. 106 below.

ibid.

34.   f. 24   Quare ut ait B' in persona Uirginis ad Iudeos, si non placet
compati filio compatimini matri.   Anglice:

Wy haue ȝe no reuthe on my child?

Index and Suppl. 4159.   RL XIV, 60.   For discussion of possible sources in
B[ernard's] Quis dabit (PL CLXXXII, col. 1136) and in AH XX, 199.8b, see
Woolf, pp. 249-50.

De Benediccione

35.   f. 24^v He þat alle þing doth wel,

His preyȝere is herd eueridel.

Tota die laudat qui omnia bene agit.

Attributed in the ms. to Augustine; cf. Enarratio in Psalmum xxxiv,
PL XXXVI, col. 341.

8

ibid.

36.   f. 24^v Blissed moten þo pappes be

                  Þat Godes sone sok of þe.

                  Benedicta sint vbera que lactauerunt Christum.

Cf. 'Beata ubera tua, quæ lactaverunt Christum Dominum' (Anselm, Oratio lviii, 'Ad Sanctam Virginem Mariam', PL CLVIII, col. 963); and more generally AH XXXI, 147 and 148 ('De Uberibus BMV'); and see Woolf, pp. 34-35.

De Beatitudine

37.   f. 25   Pore and hungri þat han nede,

                  Debonere, chaste, and reuful man,

                  Pesible and wo for her misdede:

                  Þese solen þe blisse of heuene han.

                  Pauper et esuriens, mitis, mundus, miseratus

Index 2762.   Cf. Matthew v 3-10.

ibid.

38.   f. 25

Blissed ben men pore with wil:	Beati pauperes
Heuene is here, and þat is skil:	
Blissed ben men of herte clene:	Beati mundo corde
For God almithten þei solen sene.	
Blissed ben meke men withouten strif:	Beati mites
For here sal ben þe lond of lif.	
Blissed ben þat suffren wo for rith:	Beati qui persecucionem
For heuene to hem is adith.	
Blissed ben þo þat sorwen for senne:	Beati qui lugent
For ioyȝe and mirthe þei solen winne.	
Blissed ben men þat ben ful of pes:	Beati pacifici
For Cristis children þei ben withouten les.	
Blissed ben þat hungren and þristen sothnesse:	Beati qui esurientes
For þei solen ben filled with al goodnesse.	

Index 526. Matthew v 3-10, rearranged and omitting verse 7.

De Contricione

39.   f. 25^V Into sorwe and care turned is oure pley

Versus est in luctum chorus noster ...

Index and Suppl. 221.   F.A. Patterson JEGP XX (1921) 275 (not f. 19b

and not sor wo).   Lamentations v 15-16.   English and Latin repeated

at f. 69^V, s.v. 'De Inferno', no. 92.

De Cogitacione

40.   f. 28   Senful man, ne dred þe nouth

Þou þu þenke a wikke þouth.

Ʒif þi wil is nouth þerto,

[N]e þin herte neuere þe mo,

It is þe a peine a no senne.

But betre it were for to lynne

Þan to þenken ony wikke þouth,

Woso mithte; but men may nouth.

   f. 27^V But he þat [haþ] al þis werld to calle

Forʒef vs oure sennes alle.   Amen.

Index 3111. Ne, l. 4]   Ae MS.   a(ii), l. 5: weak form of and (in

the manuscript a has a superscript mark like that used to distinguish i

amongst minims instead of a titulus to denote n; elsewhere the only written-

out form of ampersand is an).   haþ, l.9] om. MS.

ibid.

41.   f. 29   Þu man, þat wilt knowen þiself, loke quat þu hast þouth

Index 3678.   Woolf, p. 87 (wrong subject-heading, and þus not þer, l. 3).

Whiting, K100 (this ex. not noted).

De Cupiditate

42.   f. 32^V To waxen riche with gret blame

I ne make no force of no schame.

Ditari nitor; non curo quomodo ditor.`

Index 3783 (the next four couplets, nos. 43, 44, and 45 are included

under this number).

10

ibid.

43. f. 32^v He makt himself in gret richesse

Hic bene se ditat, qui semper inania vitat.

Couplet. <u>Suppl</u>. 1140.5. <u>Initia</u> 7859, <u>Sprichw</u>. 10819; only one Latin
line in Grimestone.

ibid.

44. f. 32^v Woso wile in soule hauen blisse

Of werdis godis he take þe lesse.

For þe more þat a mannis good waxit,

Þe rediere fro God is loue lessit.

Absit ditari, qui se wult mente beari

<u>Suppl</u>. 4150.3.   <u>Sprichw</u>. 171.

ibid.

45. f. 32^v Neuere to ȝelden and euere to crauen

Couplet.   <u>Suppl</u>. 2289.5. By the side is the note <u>Tullius</u> <u>de</u> <u>beneficiis</u>.
I have not traced an exact source in Seneca's <u>De</u> <u>beneficiis</u>.

ibid.

46. f. 32^v Cupiditas est:

A fals beginningge,

A dredful kepingge,

And a reuli partingge.

<u>Suppl</u>. 33.6.

De Caritate

47. f. 33^v Charite is brithe of word;

Charite is milde of mod;

Charite hat enuie non;

Charite dot no wikke won;

Charite ne louet no proud bering;

Charite desiret non heyȝing;

Charite ne sekit nout is owen wil;

Charite ne gremit nout withouten skil;

Charite ne þinket non euel þouth;

Charite of wikke ne ioyȝet nouth;

Charite þe soþe louet an weret;

Charite alle þingge oberet;

Charite leuet al þat is rith;

Charite hopet þat God hat hith;

Charite suffret alle þingge;

Charite lestet withouten endingge.

Caritas paciens est, beningna [sic] est, etc.

Index 593. I Corinthians xiii 4-8. oberet, l. 12: Vulgate suffert;
see MED s.v. aberen v.2.

De Colore

48. f. 35 Nota quod color albedo quatuor habet in se condiciones

propter quas consciencie munde comparari potest:

He taket oþer coloures arith

And oþere coloures sewith to mannis sith.

Hit sewith defaute to eueri with,

And openliche it sewith lith.

Est enim albedo:

Aliorum colorum optime receptiua

De Confessione

49. f. 36^V Quilibet debet dicere confessori sic; vulgariter sic:

f. 37 þat I, wrecche, þat senful was,

Mouwe fynde merci and cum to gras

After þis day nou wil I blinne

Forwarde maken with dedli senne.

Responsio confessoris

Hold forwarde and be stedefast,

And þin is þe blisse þat euere sal lest.

Vt veniam miser, adueniam de crimine fedus,

Non feriam post hanc, feriam cum crimine fedus.

Index 3277.

De Condicione Puerorum

50. f. 38^V Children ben litel, brith and schene, and eþe for to fillen,

Suetliche pley3ende, fre of 3ifte, and eþe for to stillen.

Sicut pueri parui, puri, paruo saciati,

Ludunt conformes, cito dant, cito pacificantur.

De Cruce

51. f. 40ᵛ   Crux est:

A barge to beren fro depe groundes,

A targe to weren fro detly woundes,

A falle to taken in þe fend,

And an halle to glaþen in a frend.

Index 23.

De Carnalitate

52. f. 40ᵛ   ȝungþe ne can nouth but leden me wil,

Ne elde ne wil nouth techen me skil.

But sum time ȝingþe beginnet a play

Þat elde ne can nouth putten away.

þerfore assone as men ben of age

Wil is a meister and skil but a page.

Index 4286. me (l. 1): = 'my'.

ibid.

53. f. 40ᵛ   ȝef ȝe liuen after þe flesses red,

He sal ȝou bringgen to det withouten dred.

Si secundum carnem vixeritis moriemini.

Romans viii 13.

De Corpore Christi

54. f. 42   Iesu, my suete with

Index 1737. R.H. Robbins MP XXXVI (1938-9) 345.

ibid.

55. f. 43   He þat is king of alle londis

At soper sith among hem tuelue,

Himself hat betuixen is hondis.

He is þat mete þat fetȝ himselue.

Rex sedet in mensa turba cinctus duodena

Initia 16778, Sprichw. 26863.

ibid.

56.　f. 43　　　Hoc est corpus meum

þis is my bodi, als ȝe mov se,

þat for ȝou sal peined be.

The ms's reference is not to one of the Gospel instances of the Latin but to I Corinthians xi (24).

ibid.

57.　f. 43　　　Effectus corpus Christi digne sumentibus:

It strengþit man in is fiting

Aȝenis felle fon.

It fillit man in is eting

With graces mani on.

It helit man of is seknesse

And kepit him fro deyȝing.

It bringet man to gret suetnesse

And to ioyȝe withouten ending.　　Amen.

digne appears to have an otiose titulus.

De Detraccione

58.　f. 45ᵛ　　　To eueri preysing is knit a knot.

þe preysing wer good, ne wer þe 'but'.

I ne woth neuere wer it may ben founde

þat with sum 'but' it is ibounde.

Cf. Chaucer's Parson's Tale X 493-4, and for this sb. use of but see MED s.v. but n.(3).

ibid.

59.　f. 45ᵛ　　　Aȝen my felawes þat I haue spoken,

And with my tungge wroth hem wo.

In endeles fir it is nou wroken.

Allas, þat euere spak I so.

Lingua calet igne, iam inheret morsibus ori

De Decepcione

60.   f. 46^{v} Manie ȝeres ben iwent

                        Si þen treuthe outȝ of londe is lent.

                        Faire wordis and wikke dede

                        Begilen man in al is nede.

                        Multis annis iam transactis, nulla fides est in pactis

Index 2095. Initia 11396, Sprichw. 15497. The Latin source is printed in RL XV, p. 346 in a discussion of poems with this topic.

ibid.

61.   f. 46^{v} Þei ben nouth wel for to leuen

See above, f. 13, no.14.

ibid.

62.   f. 46^{v} Late lef him þat michel spekt

See above, f. 13, no. 15.

ibid.

63.   f. 46^{v} Wordes ben so knit with sinne

                        Tis strong to knowen a þouth withinne.

                        Go to Treuthe and dem orith,

                        Þat senne hat tunge and hertis mith.

De Dileccione

64.   f. 47   He þat louet is frend and fo

See above, f. 19^{v}, no. 28.

ibid.

65.   f. 48   Nota quod vera dileccio debet esse:

                        Trewe withouten quey[n]tise and feiningge;

                        Lestingge withouten deceyte and chaungginge;

                        Kinde withouten hope of werdli winningge;

                        And clene withouten enticing to sinningge.

                        Vera sine simulacione dupplicitatis

queyntise] queytise MS.

15

ibid.

66.   f. 48   þei þat ben trewe in louingge,

Alone in God is here restingge.

Fideles in dileccione acquiescent ei.

Wisdom iii 9.

De Diuiciis

67.   f. 48ᵛ   It is doute in mannis richesse

Wer mo louen his godis or is worþinesse.

Cum quis positus in prosperitate diligitur, incertum valde

est vtrum possessor vel prosperitas diligatur.

Unidentified in ms., but from Gregory, Moralium Liber VII cap. xxiv,

PL LXXV, col. 781 (with some verbal changes).

ibid.

68.   f. 49   ӡef þi godis wil it ben þine,

þat after þi detӡ þu haue no pine.

Da tua, dum tua sunt: post mortem tunc tua non sunt.

Sprichw. 4861.   Whiting, M59 (this ex. not noted); cf. no. 91 below.

ibid.

69.   f. 49   Woso wile ben riche and hauing,

He fallet in þe fendes fonding.

Nam qui diuites volunt fieri ...

I Timothy vi 9.

ibid.

70.   f. 49   Betre is þe pore in his si[m]plesse

þan þe riche þat liuet with vnrithfulnesse.

Melior est pauper ambulans in simplicitate sua ...

Proverbs xix I.   simplesse] siplesse MS.

De Doctrina Sine Gracia

71.   f. 49ᵛ   Tu qui habes curam animarum tripliciter debes eas pascere

et custodire, videlicet:

þoru suetnesse of lore in preching,

þoru fair conuersacioun in leuing,

þoru ӡefte of elmesse in fynding.

Per dulcedinem doctrine in predicando

72.   f. 49ᵛ   Comet, ȝe children, me for to heren;

                   þe dred of God I sal ȝou leren.

                   Venite, filii, audite me ...

Psalm xxxiii 12.

De Delectacione

73.   f. 50   Delectacio assimilatur:

                   To þe flour springende,

                   To þe foul singende,

                   To þe deu fallende,

                   To þe snow meltende.

Cf. Suppl. 3743.6 and no. 84 below.

De Eleemosyna

74.   f. 51   þe ȝefte faliȝet nouth with skil

                   þerquiles þe herte is of good wil.

                   Nuncquam est manus vacua munere dum mens impletur bona

                   voluntate.

Gregory, XL Homiliarum in Evangelia Libri Duo, I. Homilia v, PL LXXVI,
col. 1094 (with some verbal changes). English and Latin repeated at
f. 51ᵛ, no. 75.

75.   f. 51ᵛ   þe ȝifte of hand faliȝet nout with skil

See above, no. 74.

76.   f. 52   Suich semblant Crist sal maken to þe aboue

                   Suich as þu makest her nou for his loue.

                   Tali wultu respiciet te Dominus, ea que facis cum quali facis.

De Ebrietate

77.   f. 53ᵛ   Drunkenchipe brekt

                   Al þat wisdom spekt.

                   Ebrietas frangit, quicquid sapientia tangit.

Initia 5059, Sprichw. 6874. Whiting, D420 (this ex. not noted).

De Fidelitate

78. f. 54^v Longingge, likingge, lestingge an reuthe

Schewede þat in loue was miche treuthe. Ihesus

De Fatuitate

79. f. 56^v Dred and loue, hate an good

Turnen mannis with and maken him wod.

Quatuor ista: timor, odio, dileccio, census

Initia 15330, Sprichw. 23692.

De Gradibus

80. f. 58 Nota 12 gradus humilitatis secundum Bernardum in libro de

12 gradibus. Anglice:

Ber þe wel an quemfuliche.

Spek seldom and skilfuliche.

Ne lauque nouth to lithliche.

Ne ansuere nouth to rediliche.

Fulfil þe comandemens treuliche.

Dispise þeself inwardliche.

Seu þi fautes openliche.

Suffre penaunce mildeliche.

Hold þe vnworþi to don oniþing.

To þin hey3ere be vnderling.

þin owen wil þu fulfille nouth.

To louen God for3ett et nouth.

3ef þu wilth ben meke sothliche,

Fulfil þese þinges bisiliche.   Amen.

Sit bona et placita tua conuersacio

Index and Suppl. 480. The ms's reference to B' is presumably to Bernard's
De Gradibus Humilitatis, but the Latin equivalent of the English has not
been traced.

De Gracia

81. f. 58 Man ne hat nouth grace for God 3ef hit nouth,

But for it is nouth rediliche of man isouth.

Homo non habet graciam non quia hanc non dat Deus.

Attributed in the ms. to Anselm.

ibid.

82.   f. 58ᵛ   Wanne þe sunne rist:
                  þe day taket his lith,   Misericordia
                  þeues taken here flith,   Demones
                  þe deu ginnet springge,   Gracia
                  [...   singge (?)]   [...]
Margin shaved.

De Gloria Mundi

83.   f. 60ᵛ   Werdis ioyȝe is menkt with wo;
                  He is more þan wod þat trostet þerto.
                  Werdis gile is wol michil;
                  þerfore it is boþe fals an fikil.
                  þe werd passet euere mo,
                  And werdly loue dot also.
Index 4225. Whiting, W671 (this ex. not noted); cf. here nos. 19, 103, and 237).

ibid.

84.   f. 60ᵛ   Gloria mundi est:
                  Als a se flouwende,
                  Als a skiȝe pasende,
                  Als þe sadwe in þe vndermel,
                  And als þe dore turnet on a quel.
Index 327. Cf. Suppl. 105.5 and no. 73 above. sadwe: faint titulus over the e ?

De Gloria Eterna

85.   f. 61   I am blisse of michil lith
                  To hem þat leden here lif orith.

De Humilitate

86.   f. 64   Be lou and louende;
                  Be meke and murnende;
                  þenk eyȝe and lok lowe;
                  Be seldum sowen and litel knowe;
                  Often scrif þe and go clene,
                  And þ[u] salt han blisse withouten wene.
Index 468. þu] þan MS.

De Hostibus

87.   f. 64ᵛ   Hoc debet diligere, videlicet:

God ouer alle þingge,

Himself withouten wemme of senningge,

His euene-Cristene as kinde þe wile teche,

þi fo withouten wiling of oni wreche.

ibid.

88.   f. 64ᵛ   Contra istos quatuor sunt quatuor hostes, videlicet:

Diabolus, þoru pride of herte and heynesse,

Caro, with lust, likingge, and vnclennesse,

Mundus, with is wrenchis and is welis-ȝerningge,

Et malus homo, with enuie, wrau werd, and bacbitingge.

welis-: = 'riches' (OED Weal, sb.¹); wrau: = 'angry' (OED Wraw, a.).

De Ingratitudine

89.   f. 68ᵛ   Wil þu art in welthe and wele

þu salt hauen frendis fele.

Ȝef þu be pore and falle in wo

Alle þi frendis wilen fro þe go.

Tempore felici multi tibi numerantur amici

Sprichw. 31228.   Cf. Whiting, P295 and P335.

ibid.

90.   f. 69   Ihesu Crist and al mankende

Dampnen þe man þat is vnkende.

And skil þat hat ben her aforn

Hat weiled þat euere was he born.

Lex et natura, Christus, simul omnia iura

Dampnant ingratum, plangunt illum fore natum.

Sprichw. 13700.

ibid.

91.   f. 69   Be þe wel, be þe wo, be þeself mynde

þat þu dost quiles þu liues, þat saltu fynde.

Children ben rekles and wyues vnkinde,

And seketourus ben fikele and taken þat he finde.

Whiting, M59 (not noted here); cf. no. 68 above.

De Inferno

92.   f. 69^v To sorwe and to care turned is my pley

See above, f. 25^v, no. 39.   The chief difference between the texts
is that f. 25^v's lst. pers. pl. pronoun is here sg.

ibid.

93.   f. 69^v Oure peynes ben grille and felle.

                           Be war of þe pit of helle.

De Iuramento

94   f. 70^v Lawe an los and rich, worchipe and of lore drede,

                           And defaute of rith, maket man to sueren in nede.

                           Lex et fama, fides, reuerencia, caucio dampni,

                           Defectus veri, tibi dant iurare licenter.

De Ieiunio

95.   f. 75   þat fastingge withouten elmesse is of mith

                           As is þe lampe with ˆoten´ olie and lith.

                           Tale est ieiunium sine eleemosyna qualis sine oleo lucerna.

Attributed in the ms. to Augustine, but untraced there; it occurs in
Isidore, Sermo I, PL LXXXIII, col. 1220.

De Lege

96.   f. 76^v Lawe is leyd vnder graue,

                           For þe demeres hand hat idrawe.

                           For þe wich hand-drawing

                           Lawe is withseth in prisuning.

                           Lex est defuncta,quia iudicis est manus vncta,

                           Ob cuius vnguentum lex est in carcere tentum.

Initia 10275, Sprichw. 13695. hand hat idrawe, hand-drawing: the Latin
indicates that bribery was involved (on the grease metaphor see J.A. Yunck
The Lineage of Lady Meed (Notre Dame 1963) pp. 196-7 and 249), but the
precise sense of the English is unclear. An intransitive sense 'to take
(money)' may serve (cf. MED s.v. drauen v., 2d. (a) 'To get (sth.), obtain';
DOST s.v. Draw, v. 9.b. 'To get into one's hands; to acquire'). Alternat-
ively, draw perhaps suggests a turning aside from the straight path, and
expresses the opposite of with even hand = 'impartially' (one and the same
example cited by MED from Mannyng's Handlyng Synne s.v. even adj.,
8. (a), and hond (e n., 1a.(e)). Such accusations were conventional (see

J.A. Yunck, op.cit., passim, and R.H. Robbins MLN LXX (1955) 473–4)
but for references to judicial scandals see W.S. Holdsworth A History of
English Law (3rd ed. London 1923) pp. 294–9.

De Luxuria

97.   f. 76^V Quil men and wemmen woniȝen togidere

þe fendes brond sone comet þidere.

Si cum viris femine habita[n]t incendiarium diaboli non deȝrit.

Attributed in the ms. to Jerome.   habitant] titulus om. MS.

ibid.

98.   f. 77   Ȝe þat wilen heuene winne,

Withdrau ȝou fro flesli senne.

Abstineatis vos ab omni fornicatione.

I Thessalonians iv 3.

ibid.

99.   f. 78   Ȝif þu wilt flen lecherie,

Fle time and stede and cumpanie.

Ȝif þu fle, senne folwith nouth;

Ȝif þu vnbide, sche comth vnsouth.

Si Venerem vitare velis, loca, tempora fuge;

Si venis tempora venit, si fugis tempora fugit.

Initia 18059, Sprichw. 29346.

ibid.

100.   f. 79^V Luxuria:

Is a robour of rentis and londis;

It is a prisoun of stronge bondis;

It is a front of sorwe and care;

And it is a swerd þat wil nout spare.

ibid.

101.   f. 80   Softeliche senne gennet in wende,

But it bitet as a neddere at þe ende.

Ingreditur blande; set in nouissimo mordebat vt colub[er].

Proverbs xxiii 31–32.   coluber] colub MS (margin shaved).

De Lingua

102.   f. 80   Als a clerk withnesset of wisdom þat can:

Herte of tunge meister is, as man of womman,

þat þe tunge no word speken ne sulde

But as þe herte assentede and seyde þat he wolde.

Cor lingue capud est sicud uir femine

De Leticia Huius Mundi

103.   f. 81   Allas, allas, þis werdis blisse lestet but a stounde;

þe laste hende þeroffe with sorwe is ibounde.

Whiting, W671 (this ex. not noted); cf. here nos. 19, 83, and 237.

De Multiloquendo

104.   f. 83ᵛ   Зif þu wilt nouth here, but spekt wordis manie and veyne,

Betre þu were to han on ere and mouþes to haan tweyзe.

For to eres God vus зaf, and mouth ne зaf but on.

[Heren michil] and speken litel becomet wel ich wis man.

Cum nihil auscultes, set plurima vana loquaris

Initia 3690a.   Heren michil] deduced from tops of letters (margin shaved);

Latin: Nos audire decet plurima pauca loqui. Whiting, E6 (this ex.

not noted).

De Misericordia

105.   f. 84ᵛ   Hem þat ben naked зif cloþing;

Hem þat ben hungri зef feding;

Mak hem beddis þat hauet nouth;

And visite þat ben in seknesse brouth;

Mak pes þer is wrethe an fith;

[. . .   ]

Vestire nudos

Margin shaved.   þat (l. 4): reading uncertain through ms. alteration.

ibid.

106.   f. 85   Lord Iesu, þin ore

Index 1965.   R.H. Robbins MP XXXVI (1938–9) 346.

ibid.

107.   f. 85   Merci abid an loke al day

Index 2155.   RL XIV, 61.

De Murmuracione

108. f. 85^v   Drau þe neuere to man

þer is lif is wan.

Nulli se iungʒit [sic], sua quem discordia pungit.

Initia 12382, Sprichw. 18996.

De Morte

109. f. 86   Sort arn mennis dayʒes; his monis ben told also;

His termis ben iseetʒ þat he ne may ouergo.

Breues dies hominis sunt; numerus mensium, etc.

Job xiv 5.

ibid.

110. f. 86^v   Mors

Be war, man, I come as þef

To reuen þi lif þat is þe lef.

Suppl. 517.5. Woolf, p. 337, prints this tag and the next triplet (no.111) as one poem; the transcript of both has errors.

ibid.

111. f. 86^v   Mors:

It is bitter to mannis mende;

It is siker to mannis kende;

It is delere of al oure ende.

See above, no. 110. This triplet, marked as a separate poem in the manuscript, is not spoken by Death, but is a characterization of it. For this kind of definition poem cf. that on Lust, no. 100.

ibid.

112. f. 87   Mors habet quatuor litteras, videlicet DETH, et possunt designari quatuor condiciones mortis. Nam per D:

Deth is a Dredful Dettour;

Deth is an Elenge hErbergour;

Deth is a Trewe Tollere;

And Deth is an Hardi Huntere.

24

ibid.

113.   f. 87   It doth harm, and hat don harm,

To putten forth þe time.

He þat kepth him nouth to-day fro harm

To-morwen may gon to pine.

Et nocet et nocuit semper differre paratis;

Qui non est hodie cras minus aptus erit.

For l. 1 of Latin cf. Sprichw. 17080b; l.2 is Sprichw. 24398.

ibid.

114.   f. 87   He þat time borwith fro morwe to morwen,

And ȝelth with þe mouth,

He sal han ned to borwen to-day or to-morwen

A word of his mouth.

ibid.

115.   f. 87   Watso þu art þat gost her be me

Si quis eris qui transieris, sta, respice, plora

G.R. Owst Preaching in Medieval England (Cambridge 1926) p. 344.

ibid.

116.   f. 87   With a sorwe and a clut

Al þis werd comet in and out.

ibid.

117.   f. 87   On mo[r]ewe morwen comet al oure care

Wan borwed ware wil hom fare.

morewe] monewe MS; morewe morwen = 'tomorrow morning' (cf. DOST s.v.

Morow, Morrow, n., 2.d. The morrow morning, lst. rec. 1662; and cf. here

the theme of nos. 113, 124, and 140.

ibid.

118.   f. 87   Ȝef preyȝer or mede

Mith of Detȝ maken meistre,

þoru preyȝere or mede

Man of Detȝ sulde be fre.

Si prece vel precio potuisset Mors superare

ibid.

119. f. 87   Haue detȝ in mende:

Neuere sal senne þi soule schende.

ibia.

120. f. 87   Riche and pore, ȝung and old,

þerquiles ȝe hauen ȝure with in wol lde] ,

Seket soule bote;

For wan ȝe wenen al þerbest

To hauen helþe, pes an rest,

þe ex is at þe rote.

Index 2817.   Stanza from The Proverbs of Hending; see G. Schleich Anglia

LI (1927) 268-9.   wolde] wo MS (margin shaved).   Whiting, A253 (not noted

here).
ibid.

121. f. 87^V   Man wenit euere for to liuen;

He þinket nouth þat he sal deyȝe.

þoru det adoun he sal ben driuen,

And ben begiled in is eyȝe.

Vir vitam querit;   non sentit quod morietur.

Morti sternetur;   sic homo falsus erit.

Index 2083.   begiled in is eyȝe: = 'deceived';   cf. bleren the eie = 'to

hoodwink, deceive, make a fool of' (see MED s.v. eie n. (1).4.(c), and

bleren v. (1). 2.).

ibid.

122. f. 87^V   Sey, þu vessel of wrechidnesse,

Wat profitet þe werdis richesse?

In a dep pitȝ doun to þe kne,

Sken and bon, men solen closen þe.

Dic homo, vas scelerum, quid prodest copia rerum?

In modica fossa clauderis, pellis et ossa.

Suppl. 3079.3.

26

ibid.

123. f. 87^V Man is but a frele þing

Fro þe time of is genning.

Nou he is an nou [e] nis,

Als þe flour þat springet in gres.

Est homo res fragilis, et durans tempore paruo

Suppl. 2066.8. Initia 5691, Sprichw. 7486. e, l. 3] en MS; e = 'he'
(Latin: Nunc est, nunc non est).

ibid.

124. f. 87^V Alle we liuen hapfuliche;

No man ne trost wan he sal deyȝe.

þerfore ne tak nouth wrongfuliche,

For peraunter to-morwe þu gost þi weyȝe.

Viuimus hic sorte; noli spem ponere morte

Suppl. 230.5.

ibid.

125. f. 87^V Siker is det to alle maner men;

To tellen of is time neuere no man kan.

Mors cunctis certa, nihil est incertius hora.

Suppl. 3100.5 (errors in transcript). Sprichw. 15123; only one Latin line
in Grimestone. Whiting, D96.

ibid.

126. f. 87^V Sey nou, man, quat þinkest þu

þat hast þis werd to wille?

þou al þis werd wer þin rith nou,

A litel herde sal þe fulfille.

Dic, homo, quid speres, qui mundo totus inheres

Suppl. 3078.5. Initia 4363, Sprichw. 5559.

ibid.

127. f. 87^V Homo in fine

His colour blaket

Index and Suppl. 1220. R.H. Robbins Mediaeval Studies XXXII (1970) 295.

ibid.

128.　f. 87^v　　Her sal I duellen, loken vnder ston

Hic habitabo, clausus in tumulo

Suppl. 1210.5.　Woolf, p. 88.

ibid.

129.　f. 87^v　　Si fas esset loqui, quilibet mortuus possit dicere 'Heu'

propter quatuor:

For I ham pore, withouten frendes,

In gret pine among þe fendis,

Wirmis mete day and nith,

To hard rekning I am dith.

Suppl. 825.8.

ibid.

130.　f. 87^v　　Herde maket halle,

And herde maket bour;

Herde reyset castel

And herde reyset tour.

Wan herde is leyd in herde,

Blac is his bour;

Þan sal herde for herde

Hauen many a bitter sour.

Wan herde hat herde

Wonnen with wo,

And herde hat herde

Loken in his clo,

And herde hat of herde ·

loyȝe rith inow,

Þan sal herde bewepen

Þat he [iʒ] eer below.

Index 703.　sour, l. 8: perhaps an error for stour (see OED s.v. Stour,

sb.^{1}, 2).　clo, l. 12: = 'claw', 'grasp'.　is, l. 16] om. MS.

De Mundo Fugiendo

131.   f. 90^v   Quatuor tortores hominis in mundo, videlicet:

þe werd with is faired

þat benemet man is sith;

þe man with is falsed

þat benemet man is mith;

þe fles with hire tendred

þat reuet man is with;

þe deuel with is leþered

þat hem alle togidre knith.

Index 3505.

De Nouis

132.   f. 91^v   Deth is lif: id est, mors Christi est vita nostra, etc.

Pes his strif: qui enim habet pacem habet cum corpore

discordiam.

Sorth is long: id est, modica penitentia hic longa est

quantum ad vitam.

And feble is strong: qui enim prius debiles fuerunt in

resistendo, iam fortes facti sunt

in perficiendo.

De Oracione

133.   f. 93   Nout mannis steuene but good wille,

Nout mirthe of mout but herte stille,

Non loud cri ne non hey lay

But priue bidding is Godis pay.

Non vox set votum, non musica cordula set cor

Index 2298 (note Latin also accompanies Grimestone text).   Another

version is printed by T. Silverstein Medieval English Lyrics (London 1971),

no. 51, from another Franciscan compilation, the Fasciculus Morum, s.v.

I vii, 'De Membris Superbie' (Bodley MS Rawlinson C. 670).   Initia 12222,

Sprichw. 18723.   The Latin agrees in all four lines with Silverstein's.

ibid

134. f. 95   þe þanne, we beseken, þi seruans do good,

                 þe wiche þat þu bouthtest with þi dere blod.

                 Te ergo quesumus famulis tuis subueni quos precioso sanguine

                 redimisti.

Suppl. 3510.5.   From the Te Deum.

ibid.

135. f. 95   Pater Noster

                 Oure fader, þat art in heuene onon,

                 Iblissed be þi name.

                 þi kingdam come.   þi wil be don

                 In heuene and herde isame.

                 Oure daiȝes bred grant vus þis day.

                 And forȝef vus oure blame

                 As we forȝeuen oure fomen ay

                 þat don vus wo or schame.

                 But, Iesu, for þi michil mith,

                 þu suffres nouth to falle

                 In fonding of þe fendes mith,

                 But fro harm þu child vus alle.

Index 2708.

De Obediencia

136. f. 96   It is wol lithliche iborn

                 þer good wil wilcomet beforn.

                 þat he doth aȝen his wil,

                 It semet hard with rith an skil.

                 Portatur leuiter, quod portat quisque libenter

Sprichw. 21951 (only one line).

ibid.

137. f. 97   Totum interius se colligit vt imperantis in se colligat

                 voluntatem. Anglice:

                 Eyne to seing;

                 Eres to hering;

                 Tunge to speking;

Hondis to werching;

Feet to going.

Oculos parat visui [subject is <u>obediens</u>, the obedient man]

Attributed in the ms. to Jerome.

De Ocupacione

138.   f. 98   Sorfulhed of detȝ þat stant an waitet þe;

Reufulhed of Cristes blod þat schad was on þe tre;

Hidoused of helle fir þat brennet withouten ende;

Blisfulhed of heuene lith þat mad is for mankende.

Mors tua, mors domini, fraus mundi, gloria celi

Et dolor inferni sint meditanda tibi.

<u>Initia</u> 11275, <u>Sprichw</u>. 15210.

ibid.

139.   f. 98   Woso þouthte of his birthe

And wider he sal wende,

He sulde neuere maken mirthe,

But sorwe withouten ende.

Si quis sentiret, quo tendit, et vnde veniret

<u>Initia</u> 17947, <u>Sprichw</u>. 29074.

ibid.

140.   f. 98   Bisiliche ȝef þe to lore

Als þu suldest liuen eueremore.

But fle senne in ich a play

As to-morwen sulde ben þi ded-day.

Viue vacans studio, quasi numquam sis moriturus

<u>Sprichw</u>. 33957. English and Latin repeated at f. 154^v, s.v. 'De Tempore',

no. 236.

De Oculo

141.   f. 99^v   Disputacio inter cor et oculum

Dicit cor oculo

þu schendest me sore with þi loking

<u>Index</u> 3690.   C. Brown MLN XXX (1915) 198.

De Peccato

142. f. 101ᵛ   Peccator assimilatur:

To a fals tresorer,

To a fals herberger,

To a puttok fleyȝende,

And to a weþerkoc turnende.

ibid.

143. f. 103   Fle þe dich of senne

þat þu fal nouth þerinne.

Tu caueas caueas, ne perias per eas.

Sprichw. 31617.

ibid.

144. f. 103ᵛ   After þat þe appel was eten withouten detȝ passed non of alle.

Allas for þat wrecched hap þat to mankinde was falle.

ibid.

145. f. 104   Peccatum est vitandum propter quatuor: For it is

A filthe þat God almithten hateȝ,

A foul sting þat is angeles wlateȝ,

A wikke ded þat þe deuel liketȝ,

A sori euel þat þis werd beswyketȝ.

ibid.

146. f. 104ᵛ   Pro vetito pomo corruit omnis homo

For þat appel þat Eue tok

Al mankindde Crist forsok.

Virginis et merito iam regnabit homo

And þoru Maries rithfulnesse

Nu we ben alle siker of blisse.

ibid.

147. f. 104ᵛ   Ne bring þu nouth þeself to lowe

With lust þat lestet but litel þrowe.

For werdis lust doth heuene tine

And leth þe nexte weyȝe to pine.

Nulli confundi misera dulcedine mundi

Initia 11899a, Sprichw. 17089.   þu, I. 1] or þe (last letter obliterated).
leth: = 'leadeth'.

32

ibid.

148. f. 104^v Quilibet peccator potest dicere 'Amen':

A   Allas for sennes þat I haue wrouth;

M   Merci, Iesu, þat hast me bouth;

E   Elp, Ihesu, an saue þu me.

N   Nede maket me criȝen to þe.

ibid.

149. f. 104^v Woso louet nouth to don orith,

Treuliche he hatit lith.

Qui male agit, odit lucem.

Sprichw. 24207a.

De Pace

150. f. 105^v Pes be

In vertu of þe.

Fiat pax in virtute tua.

Psalm cxxi 7.

De Periculo

151. f. 108^v Tria versantur cotidie in periculo, videlicet:

þe schip in þe seyling,

Treuthe in michil speking,

And chastete in þe werd duelling.

Nauis in pelago

ibid.

152. f. 108^v Wan þu makst ingong,

Beþenk þe so to ben þolmod,

þat at þin outgong

No man sey of þe but good.

Qui facis ingressum, studeas sic esse modestus

Sprichw. 24069.

De Paupertate

153. f. 112 þe pore man oueral liȝ stille

Quil is pours is nouth at is wille.

Pauper vbique iacet, dum sua bursa tacet.

Sprichw. 20949.

De Passione Christi

154.   f. 117   With it was his naked brest, and red is blodi side

Candet nudatum pectus ...

Index and Suppl. 4088.   RL XIV, p. 241 (also prints Latin source).   The
Latin, attributed in the manuscript to Augustine (see PL XL, col. 906),
is now identified as the work of John of Fécamp;   see Woolf, p. 28.
Another translation occurs at f. 120, no. 179.

ibid.

155.   f. 117   Man, siker helpe hast þu and prest

Index and Suppl. 2074.   Woolf, p. 34.   For possible sources in Arnold of
Bonneval and Stephen of Sawley see Woolf, p. 34.

ibid.

156.   f. 118^V   Hou hard it was, and wat distresse,

My detʒ þe sewith þis liknesse.

Þus dere I haue þoru my godnesse

Bouth mankende fro wrechednesse.

Mors mea quam dura fuit, indicat ista figura

Initia 11257;   two Latin lines in Grimestone.

ibid.

157.   f. 118^V   Seth faste þi fot on rode-tre;

In Cristis bodi mak þi se;

Drau adoun a bou to þe,

A froit of loue þer mauth ise.

In cruce fige pedem, de Christo fac tibi sedem;

Frondes carpe tibi, fructus amoris ibi.

ibid.

158.   f. 118^V   Spere and cros, nail, detʒ and þorn

Schewen hou I bouthte man þat was forlorn.

Lancea, crux, claui, mors, spine, quam tolleraui

Initia 10100, Sprichw. 13434a.

ibid.

159.   f. 118^V   Hand, heued, foot, herte

Criʒet Crist for wondis smerte.

ibid.

160. f. 118^v   We ben heled þat eer wer seke.

Iblissed be þat wonder leche.

Sanati sumus.

Isaiah liii 5; attributed in ms. to 'Psalm 2'.

ibid.

161. f. 119   þus is al þe herte of man

So clenliche turned into his lemman

þat on þe lemes þat ben withoute

þe loue springet al aboute.

Sic transformatur cor amantis in id, quod amatur

Index and Suppl. 3520 (þus is not þer as, l. 1). Sprichw. 29553.

ibid.

162. f. 119   Crist criȝede wan he preyȝede forȝefnesse of oure senne;

Crist criȝede wan he þristede þe helthe of mankenne;

Crist criȝede wan he þolede harde peynes an wo;

Crist criȝede wan his soule fro þe bodi sulde go.

Index 602.

ibid.

163. f. 119   Cristis bodi maltȝ,

þe soule it sualtȝ,

þe blod was spiltȝ,

For mannis gilt.

Corpus Christi liquessebat

Index 629.   l. 2: Latin 'Anima uero recedebat'.

ibid.

164. f. 119   Christus potest dicere:

Ha 'r' de gates I haue go --

It is isene on eueri to --

To maken my frend of my fo.

Loue me, man, for al my wo.

Index 1089.

ibid.

165. f. 119   'Wo þe þus beseþ, Iesu, my suete lif?'

'For mannis soule to biȝen les I þus mi lif.'

Quis te lesit, ita Iesu, dulcissima vita

Suppl. 4110.3 (þus not þer, I. 1). Initia 16112.

ibid.

166. f. 119   He þat was al heuene with him þat al hat wrouth,

Als a wreche he hat him lowed and mad himself as nouth.

A þrallis robe þei han him taken, þat Lord of mith þat hadde

no nede.

It semet he hadde himself forsaken to ben clad in mannis wede.

Semetipsum exinaniuit, formam serui accipiens, etc.

Index 1167.   Philippians ii (6-) 7.

ibid.

167. f. 119   Reuthe made God on mayden to lithte;

Reuthe mad him comen to mannes sithte;

Reuthe mad his armis on rode sprede;

And reuthe mad him wepen and loude grede.

Index 2011.   See above, f. 19, no. 25.

ibid.

168. f. 119   Heu:

Allas, Iesu, þi loue is lorn.

Allas, Iesu, þi det is suorn.

Allas, Iesu, þi bane is born.

Index 156.

ibid.

169. f. 119   Sanguis Christi:

Is a priue pouyson

And a ferli foysoun,

Quedes for to quellen

And frendis for to fillen.

Index 1606.

ibid.

170.   f. 119   Al mi blod for þe is sched

       Couplet.   Suppl. 193.8.

ibid.

171.   f. 119   Crist lay an loude gredde,

                       His armis fro him wide spredde;

                       Blod an water longe bledde,

                       With þat blod vs alle fedde.

       Index 609.

ibid.

172.   f. 119   Apparet mihi quod facies Christi:

                       Is wan of beting,

                       Is foul of speting,

                       Is grisli of bolning,

                       An reuli of weping.

       Index 1610.

ibid.

173.   f. 119   3ef þu wilt ben strong in fith

                       An fornemen þe deuel is mith,

                       þenk hou loue dede Crist to dey3e   Amor

                       On cros mankende for to bi3e.

       Index 1436.

ibid.

174.   f. 119ᵛ   A sory beuerech it is and sore it is abouth

       Index and Suppl. 94. RL XIV, 62. The general source is found in the
previous item of two biblical references: 'Pater, si fieri possit, etc. Et
iterum, Si vis vt bibam, etc.' (cf. Mark xiv 35 and Matthew xxvi 42).

ibid.

175.   f. 119ᵛ   Ihesu God is becomen man

       Index 1714. Woolf, p. 178; ends: 'Amen'.

ibid.

176.   f. 119^v Oracio

God Lord þat sittes in trone

Index 955.   R.H. Robbins MP XXXVI (1938-9) 346 (wisdom not widsom, l. 3).

ibid.

177.   f. 119^v Ihesu

I am Iesu, þat cum to fith

Index and Suppl. 1274.   RL XIV, 63.

ibid.

178.   f. 120   Lamentacio dolorosa

Beda.   Audi cum Maria que dixit:

Suete sone, reu on me, and brest out of þi bondis

Index 3245.   RL XIV, 64.   On the source attributed to Bede see RL XIV, p. 266, and Woolf, p. 250.

ibid.

179.   f. 120   Bare was þat quite brest

Index 461.   Woolf, p. 30.   Another version of the Candet nudatum pectus: see above, f. 117, no. 154.

ibid.

180. ·f. 120   Lullay, Iullay litel child, child reste þe a þrowe

Index 2023.   RL XIV, 65.   Obertello, p. 226 (on no. 11 in his ed.) and Woolf, p. 155 n.2. argue that this lullaby is spoken not by the Virgin but by a meditator (cf. here no. 8).

ibid.

181.   f. 120^v Ihesus

Behold, womman, a dolful sith:

þis is þ[i] sone þat hanget here.

A spere myn herte hat þoru pith,

Min heued is corouned with a brere.

I þat was Lord of lif an lith

Det hat changed al my chere.

Allas þat man me hat þus dith,

To wam I was felawe and fere.

Maria

    Allas, mi sone, nou I deyʒe

    For þi pines and for þi wo.

    Myn herte ne may no lengere dreyʒe

    For þi blod þat rennet þe fro.

Index 504.   þi, l. 2] þis MS; emended by Woolf, p. 252.

ibid.

182. f. 120ᵛ   Arma Christi

    A scheld of red, a cros of grene,

    A corune of þornes wonden kene,

    A spere, a sponge, and nayles þre,

    A bodi bounden to a tre --

    Woso þis seld to him take,

    For is foman þar him nouth quake.

Index 91.   Printed from MS Bodley 622 by C. and K. Sisam The Oxford
Book of Medieval English Verse (Oxford 1970), no. 270.

ibid.

183. f. 121   'þu þat hangest þer so heyʒe,

    þu art mi sone -- I ne haue no mo.

    þu slest me with þat loueli eyʒe

    þat was so fair -- nou waxit blo.'

Ihesus

    'Moder, þou I deyʒe sore

    And suffre det with peines strongge,

    If men me kuden peyne more

    I were redi to vnderfongge.

    But for al þe loue þat may be,

    Or euere was betwixen us twyʒe,

    Hangen I wile vpon þis tre

    And for loue of man I wile her deyʒe.'

ibid.

184.   f. 121   Ihesus

Loue me brouthte

Index and Suppl. 2012.   RL XIV, 66.

ibid.

185.   f. 121   Ihesus

Maiden and moder, cum and se

Index and Suppl. 2036.   RL XIV, 67.

ibid.

186.   f. 121^V Vndo þi dore, my spuse dere

Caput meum plenum est rore (Canticum 5);   Ecce sto ad

hostium et pulso (Apocalypsis 3).

Index and Suppl. 3825.   RL XIV, 68 (margin, l. 7: Responsio peccatoris).

Canticles v 2;   Revelation iii 20;   see Woolf, p. 51 n.2.

ibid.

187.   f. 121^V Allas, wo sal myn herte slaken?

Index 162.   R.H. Robbins MLN LIII (1938) 244.

ibid.

188.   f. 121^V Crist is offred for mannis sake

Immolatus est Christus.

Couplet.   Suppl. 607.5.   I Corinthians v 7.

ibid.

189.   f. 121^V But I me bethouthte

Inderliche and ofte

Wat Crist drey for me

Withinnen and withouten,

And al a wone buten,

Wan he was on þe tre.

Wol sore I may me drede

At my moste nede

He wil forsaken me.

Index 554.

ibid.

190. f. 121ᵛ   Cristis blod, þe heyȝe of lif, þre þinggis it hat vndon:

Heuene, and helle, and mannis soule þat michil hat misdon.

Iche man oliue þat wile rith wel don,

þenk of þo wondes fiue, þat he ne be nout fordon.

Index 628.

ibid.

191. f. 122.   Respiciamus:

Oculis þe rede stremes renning;

Auribus þe lewes orible criȝing;

Gustu of Cristis drink þe bitternesse;

Tactu of Cristis wondis þe sarpnesse.

Suppl. 3452.8.

ibid.

192. f. 122   Oracio bona

Mi Lord, with herte I preyȝe þe, withouten vois wol stille

Index 2258 (the item, ending 'Amen', consists of one couplet, and not

four lines as stated by Index and as printed by R.H. Robbins MP XXXVI

(1938-9) 346 who includes no. 193).

ibid.

193. f. 122   More loue may no man schewe

Maiorem caritatem nemo habet, etc.

Couplet.   See above, no. 192.   John xv 13.

ibid.

194. f. 122   Ecclesia potest dicere

I ne may leuen on non manere,

Ne leten for no þing,

To wepen for Iesu, my lemman dere;

I murne for loue-longing.

Allas, I se him deyȝe

þat me was wone to lere.

I se him peined on fele manere;

Ihesu, wat sal I seyȝe?

Non me possum continere

Index 1336.

ibid.

195. f. 122   Behold þu, man, her myth þu se

þe armes þat I bar for þe.

On my passioun be þi mynde

þat þin enemiʒe þe idel ne fynde.

Stes, homo, respicias

Index and Suppl. 501.

ibid.

196. f. 122   Mi dere lemman, behold þu me,

Hou I hange on rode-tre.

Mi bodi is fast with nailes þre,

Mi side is. þerled for loue of þe.

On þi soule haue þu pite,

And fle senne for loue of me,

And þu salt hauen þat blissing

þat þe may ʒeuen heuene king.   Amen.

Index 2234.

ibid.

197. f. 122   þin herte with spere stiked,

þin heued with þornes priked,

þin wondis rent be note,

þin loueli heued bouwing,

þin faire bodi bleding

Merci vs hat behote.   Merci.

Index 3562.   The sense of note is obscure.

42

ibid.

198.   f. 122^v Rith as man may se
Wan child to skole set be,
A bok him is ibrouth
Nailed on a brede of tre
And is icleped an A B C,   5
Perteliche iwrouth.

Wrouth is on þe bok withoute
Fiue paraffes grete and stoute,
So red so rose schape.
þan is withinnen saun doute   10
Ful of lettres al aboute,
Boþen rede an blake.

Blake letres in þe perchemyn
Maket þe child sone afyn
Lettres to knowen an se.   15
Be þis bok men may deuyn
Cristes bodi, ful of peyn,
þat deyȝed on rode-tre.

On tre he was nailed wol bliue.
þe grete paraffes his wondis fiue   20
We moun wel vnderstonde.
Loke in is side, maiden and wiue,
Hou his fomen nailes goun driue
In fot and ek in honde.

In hond an fot him was ful wo.   25
Lettres þer weren many mo,
Withinnen and ek withoute,
With rede wondes and strokes blo.
þus was he writen fro heued to to,
His faire bodi aboute.   30

Abouten þis A B C   wold I spede,

ʒef I mithte þe lettres rede

Withouten [distaunce] .

God, þat let his bodi sprede   col. b.

On þe rode for mannis nede,   35

In heuene vs alle avaunce.

God with launce was stongen for vs.

False Iudas, to amenden his pours,

To det he had him sold.

On Gode Friday, þe clerkes seyn vs,   40

For mannis helthe ded was Ihesus:

In ston he lay al cold.

A reuful mone may man make

Hou suete Iesu Crist was take.

Lestene a litel pas.   45

þe Iewes him wrouthten miche wrake,

And ledden him with wol gret rape

Aforn þe bissop Cayphas.

Bunde he was for oure bounte,

And suffred strokes gret plente   50

Beforn Cayphas þat nith.

On ernemorwen, I telle þe,

ʒet was he beten on a tre

Beforn Pilates sith.

Cleimed and sent he was to Herrodes þe king   55

þer he hadde manie strokes and gret skorning.

He bad hem turnen here gate

And leden þe maidenes sone ʒing

For to taken his iugging

Of þe iustise, Pilate.   60

44

Dempt he was vpon a stounde
And token a cloth aş is ifounde
And wonden him þerin.
In driȝe blod wan he was wonde
Þrewen his bodi to þe grounde   65
And renten of cloth an skyn.

Euene in his eyne greyȝe   f. 123
Þe lewes spatleden, soth to seyȝe,
And ledden fort þat milde.
Marie wente ouer a feld lay leyȝe   70
To Caluari, þer Crist sulde deyȝe,
And waited þer hire childe.

For feynting fel þat faire fod,
Naked as he bar þe rod
Toward Caluary.   75
Al beronnen with red blod,
Among þe lewes wilde and wod,
He swounede sikirly.

God Lord, gret was þi pine,
Naked on rod, þat ilke time.   80
He leyden him on þe londe
To drowen is lemes holy and dingne.
Þeron he teiȝeden þe longe leygne,
And naileden fot and honde.

Harde þei houen þe heui rode;   85
His bodi heng þer al on blode,
As beret withnesse Sen Ion.
Þe cursede lewes, wilde and wode,
Pithten þe cros with egre mode
In þe morteys of ston.   90

Ihesu, with Iewes gret was þi pine;

Fot and hond, for soth to seyne,

Slit ben in þat tide,

Al to-brosten senwe an veyne,

As beret withnesse Maudeleyne --   95

Sche sau his wondis wyde.

King was clad in pore wede;

Al þe senne of mannes dede

He hat about wol dere.

To byӡen vs heuene with merie mede   col. b.   100

His suete blod he gan out schede

And after water clere.

Long loue God hadde in herte

To sauen soules. He seyde him þreste

Ner wan þe gost sulde go.   105

þe cursede Iewes, kene and querte,

Menkten eysyl with galle smerte,

And bodin him drinken þo.

Man, of pite and of merci

Maidenes sone Sey[n]te Mari   110

On Gode Friday þus deyӡede.

Naked he heng on Caluari,

With wyde wondis witterli,

A þef on eyþer side.

Nout had he in þat nede,   115

But sarpe þornes, his blod to schede,

To his crune wol faste cleued.

þo seyde Crist, soth as te Crede,

'God, þat deyӡed for mannis dede,

Hat nouth to resten on his heued.'   120

Out ran is blod brit.

þo seyde God almith

Als he heng on þe tre,

'With þe lewes so am I dith

I seme a wirm to mannis sith,   125

Mankynde, for loue of þe.'

Prikkes him peyned, as ʒe may here.

His heued was broyden with a brere,

Sothli for to sayn.

With red blod was wet his lere;   130

þe pinnes þoru his panne dere

Su[n]kken into his brayn.

Quen of heuene, wo was þe   f. 123^v

To sen hangen on rode-tre

Ihesu, þi sone so suete   135

Hire tendre herte ner brast on þre --

þis is a vers of gret pite --

Reuli teres sche wepte.

Robed he was in red blod.

þus heng he cloþed on þe rod   140

Aʒenes þe sunnes lem.

To slen oure Creature good

Egre and wilde was here mod,

þe lewes of Ierusalem.

Slith was is fles and flawe.   145

þe lewes þoru here false lawe

Deden him michel pine .

þus seyt þe Gospel in his sawe

þat eueri ioynt was to-drawe --

Men mithten sen senewe and veyn.   150

To michil schame hadde God of pris.
Iewes him setten in sorful sis,
And he seyd hem no loth.
Wan he hadden nailed oure Lord so wis,
Tweyȝe Iewes kesten at þe dis   155
Wo sulde han his cloth.

Wyde weren his wondis, al blod-wete,
From þe heued doun to his fete.
Þus, þan, was he slawe.
Þis Lombes blod oure bale gan bete,   160
Of wam þat spak manie prophete
So longe in þe Olde Lawe.

Exis þe Iewes token þat tide.
To þe þeues he gunne to glide.
Here hipes þan broken he,   165
And setten a lance to Cristis side   col. b.
And dedyn a blind knit vnbide
To cleuen is herte on þre.

Y wot wel wo sulen þey ben
Þat louen nout God þat deiȝed on tre   170
With al þis passioun.
At Domesday men sal wel se
Wo loued God with herte fre,
With gret deuocioun.

Zadliche he suffrede al þis sorwe   175
Fro þat it was ernemorwe
Til it was passed non.
His gost þan went his frend to borwe;
þe bodi heng ded with wondis corue;
þan was þis dede idon.   180

48

And is to seyʒe: God was ded;

Of is blod his bodi was red.

He ros on Esterne morwe.

Nu is he comen toforn þe qued,

And ʒeft his bodi in furme of bred   185

þat sal us alle borwe.

Siker, man, siker, siker.

Loue þu þis passion in al þi mende,

And wen þe heuene withouten ende.

      Est Amen.   190

At Domesday we solen vprise

And wenden fort, foles and wyse,

To Ebron sikerli.

And þer sal ben þe grete assise,

And God of heuene, þe hey iustise,   195

With wondis al blodi.   Ihesu, merci.

Index and Suppl. 1523 and Index 424 (ll. 191-6).   Printed from British
Museum MS Harley 3954 by F. J. Furnivall EETS OS 15 (2nd ed. 1903)
pp. 271-8.   Lines 187-9 correspond to the first three lines of Harley's
stanza 32, and ll. 191-3 correspond to the last three lines of that stanza
(which has seven lines in all); ll. 194-6 correspond to the last three lines
of Harley's st. 33; the Grimestone text has 33 stanzas (counting ll. 187-90
as a stanza) compared with Harley's 37.   For comment on the ultimate
source, Revelation v 1, and on the text of Harley see Woolf, p. 253 n.2.

N.B.   The marginal letters have not been printed.

an, 1.5: an ampersand in the manuscript, and this is elsewhere written out
only as an.   distaunce, l. 33] distraunce MS, dystaunce Harley; withouten
distaunce = 'without delay or hesitation' (see MED s.v. distaunce n. 6.(b)).
ll. 46-47] order reversed in MS.   rape, l. 47: = 'haste' (OED Rape, sb.[1]),
an inexact but perhaps permissible rhyme; Harley's rhyme word here is shake,
and cf. OED s.v. Rake, sb.[3], 2.a. 'A run, rush; speed'.   Cleimed, l. 55:
= ? 'accused'.   He, l. 57: i.e. Herod.   ll. 62, 65: the omission of the
subject pronouns, present in Harley, may have been acceptable ME idiom.
Cf. T.F. Mustanoja A Middle English Syntax (Helsinki 1960) pp. 138-44.

lay ley3e, I. 70: '(that) lay fallow or unploughed' (see OED s.v. Lea, ley, lay, a., for collocation of lea and lie (OED Lie, v.¹, 8); Harley reads 'Mary hys moder went þe weye' (I. 72). about, I. 99: = 'paid for'. þreste, I. 104: 'thirst(ed)'. Seynte, I. 110] seyte MS. soth as te Crede, I. 118]: Whiting C541 (not noted here). II. 119-20: cf. Matthew viii 20. II. 124-6: cf. Psalm xxi 7. wirm, I.125] wirm̃ MS (in addition to the titulus, there is an oblique stroke, also over the m, in a direction contrary to that used to indicate i amongst minims). Sunkken, I. 132] Sukken MS. Creature, I. 142: = 'Creator'. II. 149-5O: a reference to Psalm xxi 17-18 (Foderunt manus meas et pedes meos, dinumeraverunt omnia ossa mea); on the use of this Psalm in Crucifixion scenes see F.P. Pickering Literature and Art in the Middle Ages (London 1970) pp. 238-42. Exis, I. 163: the marginal letter is E, not X. he, I. 165] he e MS. I. 181: the marginal mark is ampersand; for EtC following Z in the alphabet see RL XV, p. 325 (note to II. 25, 26, of 101, an alphabetical devotion to the cross). I. 187: Harley's line reads: 'Loke þat we ben seker and kende' (I. 189).

ibid.

198a.	f. 123ᵛ	At Domesday we solen vprise	
	Index 424.	Printed as II. 191-6 of previous poem; see commentary above.	

ibid.

199	f. 124	þe garlond þat of þorn is wroth	Contra superbiam
		An stikid on my crune	
		With prikking hat þe blod out brouth	
		þat dot my fored frune.	
		Min her, my muth, is al bebled,	5
		Myn heued draut doun on side;	
		Loue hat me þus lowe led	
		To don awey þi pride.	

ʒif þu art wrot and with þe wreken   Contra iram

And with þi rit hand smiten --   10

Hou my rit hand is outstreken,

First bouthe in þouth to writen.

þe nailis þoru þe senwes ben rent,

Outstremet þe blod;

þe fingres ben aʒenward bent --   15

Loke, an let þi mod.

ʒif þi lift hand helde or take   Contra cupiditatem

Any þing with wrong,

Lo, my lift hand for þi sake

Is drawen out olong.   20

þe nail went in, þe blod span out,

þe fles was wonded sore;

Bare I heng, withouten clut --

Coueyte þu no more.

ʒif slauthe wil nouth suffren þe   Contra accidiam 25

In no god werk to leste,

þing þat mine feet on þe tre

With nailes weren ifeste.

þe blod out of þe wondis

Ran doun be þe ton;   30

In al my sarpe stoundis

I stod as stille as ston.

ʒif enueyʒe wil þe dere,   Contra invidiam

þink on my rith side,

Hou it was stoungen with a spere   35

And þerwith opned wyde.

Blod and water þer out ran;

Myn herte I ʒaf þe þo.

With herte—loue þu loue man,

Boþen frend an fo.   40

3if þu wilt with herte   Contra luxuriam
Of flesses lust ben purged,
þing of þe knottes smerte
Werwith I was scurged.
Mi skin was rent, my bak was toren,   45
To peler was I bunde;
I stod naked as I was born,
þe blod ran doun to grunde.

Wan I was on rode fest   Contra gulam
And my blod out suet,   50
Dri3e I was, and sore oþrest.
þo was a sponge iwet,
In galle and vinegre togidere menk[t] ,
And so he 3euen me drinke.
þi glotoni3e so sal ben wencht   55
If þu þeroffe wilt þinke.

Index 3356.   frune, l. 4: = 'frown (with pain)';   menkt, l. 53] menk MS;
wencht, l. 55: 'quenched'.

ibid.

200.   f. 124   A Iesu, þin holi heued
With sa˘rˆpe þornes is be˘weˊ3ed;
þi faire face is al bespat,
With spotele an blod is al bewat.

Fro þi crune to þi to
þi bodi is ful of peine and wo.
Lord of þi peines þat ben so suete
Lat my soule þerinne han hete.   A[men] .

Index 4221.   An extract from EL XIII, 58 (ll. 9-14, 19-20); no music
accompanies this version.   Amen] An̄ MS (two minims visible; margin
damaged).

ibid.

201.   f. 124^v   þu sikest sore
Index and Suppl. 3691.   RL XIV, 69.

52

202.   f. 124ᵛ   Senful man, beþing and se

Vide homo quid pro te pacior

Index and Suppl. 3109. RL XIV, 70.   Initia, 8401. See Woolf, pp. 37–38.

ibid.

203.   f. 124ᵛ   Gold and al þis werdis wyn

Index and Suppl. 1002. RL XIV, 71.

ibid.

204.   f. 124ᵛ   Behold, man, wat is my wo

þer I hange vpon þe tre.

Mi blod rennet to an   fro

Be eueri side þu mith wel se.

þe spere hat smiten myn herte a-to;

For loue of þe my blod is spilt.

ʒif þu wilt fro þi senne go,

Mi merci is redi quan þu wilt.

Index 494.

ibid.

205.   f. 125   Mi folk, ˋnouˊ ansuere me

Popule meus etc.

Index and Suppl. 2240.   RL XIV, 72 (þe be-tok, l. 29: the transposition
required for rhyme is marked in MS).   Micah vi 3; the Improperia or Good
Friday reproaches.

53

ibid.

206.   f. 125   Lamentacio dolorosa

Behold þe þornes myn heued han þrongen -- hou sarpe þat it

ben;

It driuen þe blod into myn eyne -- oneses ne may I sen.

Behold þe galle þe Iewes me brungen, þe bittred woso wiste;

For pite he wolde me ȝeuen drinke -- I haue so michil þriste.

Behold þe spere myn herte hat stungen, þat þoru myn herte

glod;

Min herte hat clouen and rent onsunder -- þe poynt it was

so brod.

Behold þe scurgis myn bodi han s[w]ungen þat fomet al on blod;

þe dropes droppen vpon þe grund and rennen al on flod.

Behold þe nailes my bodi han wrungyn, driuen þoru hondis and

feet;

Hondis and armis, feet an ton, ben of þe blod al wet.

Behold my bodi with cold is clungen; I didere and quake for wo;

Of cold it quaket, of wondis it is red, of strokes bleyk and blo.

Behold my bak, wat sores ben sprungen, þe cruches knottes

maden;

þus hat det meystri of me, and lif me hat forsake.

Index 499.   it ben, It driuen, II. 1, 2: for it (with be) = 'they' see

T.F. Mustanoja A Middle English Syntax (Helsinki 1960) pp. 132-3.

oneses, I. 2: 'scarcely' (OED Uneaths, adv.). swungen, I. 7] schungen

MS [the MS form is nonsense; for the association of 'scourge' and 'swing'

see EL XIII, 35 A.6, 36.7, 84.44, RL XIV, 2 A.5.]   cruches, I. 13: =

?'lacerations', 'weals'; cf. MED s.v. cracche n.(2) 'scratching, itch'.

ibid.

207.   f. 125   Ihesus

þenk, man, þi loue was dere ibouth:

For loue of werdli þing þu les et nouth.

ibid.

208.   f. 125ᵛ   Mi loue is falle vpon a may

Index 2260.   RL XIV, 73.

ibid.

209. f. 125^V Vpon þe rode I am for þe

In cruce sum pro te

Index 3846. RL XIV, p. 261 (þat þu, l. 2: marked for transposition in MS).
Initia 8884.

ibid.

210 f. 125^V A Iesu so fair an fre

Suettest of alle þinge,

Þat ful art of pite,

Of heuene and herde kingge,

þe loue þat is in þe

No man may rede ne singge.

Bliþe may þat herte be

Þat hat of þe meni[n]gge.

O amor vehemens, Iesu dulcissime

Index 7. Only vaguely based on the Latin. meningge] menigge MS.

ibid.

211 f. 125^V Ʒe þat pasen be þe weyʒe

O uos omnes qui transitis per viam.

Index and Suppl. 4263. RL XIV, 74.   Lamentations i 12.

ibid.

212. f. 125^V Ʒe suln turnen to God:

Rediliche, withouten abiding;

Holiche, withouten ony fenying;

Gladliche, withouten vnbuxumnesse;

Sadliche, withouten gret hastinesse;

Priuiliche, withouten gret criʒing;

And lestendliche, withouten ony stinting.

Suppl. 4256.5.

55

ibid.

213.   f. 126   Ihesu, suete sone dere

Ll. 7-30 of Index 1847.   RL XIV, 75.   I have followed Woolf, pp.156-7,

in taking ll. 1-6, beginning 'Ler to louen as I loue þe', as a separate poem

(no. 215 below).   However, Miss Woolf's account of the manuscript here

needs some correction: the a-column begins with 'Ihesu, suete sone dere',

and is followed in the same column by ll. 1-8 of Index 3862 (RL XIV, 76;

no. 214 below); the b-column begins with the stanza 'Ler to louen as I loue

þe', followed by the Latin tag 'Aspice, mortalis, pro te datur ostia talis'

with its translations into   French and English (no. 216 below), followed by

ll. 9-24 of Index 3862.   The cruciform mark, coloured with red, which

frequently accompanies the beginning of a new poem, stands by 'Ihesu, suete

sone dere', the first stanza of Index 3862, 'Ler to louen as I loue þe', and

the Aspice text.   However, the 'Ler to louen' stanza is also connected by a

line of red dots to the head of the a-column, which shows perhaps that some-

one regarded it as part of 'Ihesu suete'.   The text in MS Harley 7322 f. 135^V

(EETS OS 15, 2nd ed. 1903, p. 255) is discussed by Miss Woolf, pp. 156-7;

note further that the first two lines of 'Ler to louen' also appear separately

on f. 154 of the Harley MS (ibid., p. 262).

ibid.

214.   f. 126   Primus cantus

Water and blod for þe I suete

Index 3862.   RL XIV, 76.

ibid.

215.   f. 126   Ihesu

Ler to louen as I loue þe

Ll. 1-6 of Index 1847.   RL XIV, 75.   See commentary above on no. 213.

ibid.

216.   f. 126   Behold, þu wreche, withouten strif,

Quat det I suffre for þi lif.

Aspice, mortalis, pro te datur ostia talis.

Initia 1584.

De Preceptis

217. f. 128^V Haue o god in worchipe,

[. . .]k nouth is name in idelchipe,

[. . .]e wel þe haly day,

[. . . .] moder worchipe ay.

Loke þat þu sle no man,

Ne do no foly be no womman;

Loke no þing þat þu stele,

Ne non fals withnesse þat þu bere

[. . .   ].

Index and Suppl. 1129.   For other versions and the manuscript relations
see EL XIII, 23, 70, and pp. 181-2, 219-20.   The margin is damaged at
the beginning of ll. 2, 3, and 4; the shaving of the tail-margin (tops of
letters are visible) presumably accounts for the omission of the last two
commandments.

De Peccatis Mortalibus

218. f. 130^V Nostre salutis primogenita perdit elatus;   Contra superbiam

Nostre virtutis iura reddit excerebratus.

Al oure wele and al oure lif

Sum time þoru pride was forlore.

But he hat mad oure pes of strif

þat þe sarpe coroune hat for vs bore.

Iratus sepius cito pro uindicto laborat;   Contra iram

Set Christus micius pro flagellantibus orat.

A man þat is ful of wreche

Euere he seket to taken vengaunce.

But anoþer lessoun Crist gan vs teche:

He bad for is fon in his penaunce.

Cla[u]duntur denuo frequenter manus auari; Contra cupiditatem

Configunt ideo ligno claui manus amari.

Wikked þing is coueytise

þat nouth wil ȝeue but vnderfonge.

þerfore Crist at is iuwyse

Was nayled þoru honden with nailes longe.

57

Pedes torpentis ne proficiant retrahuntur;   Contra accidiam
Hinc cum tormentis pedes eius afficiuntur.
To leren oni noteful lore
Men got slauliche, as ȝe may se.
þerfore Cristes feet, wol sore,
Wer nailed to þe harde tre.

Inuidus exuritur faciem, licet hillaret
ore,   Contra inuidiam
Set cor diuiditur vt nos iungat in amore.
þe enuiouse man him is wo
Tofor men, hou so heth make.
þerfore his herte was smite a-to
To techen vs louen for his sake.

Corpus mundatum semper luxuria fedat;   Contra luxuriam
Est flagellatum corpus ne nemini ledat.
Among al oþere, lecherie
Filet man and bringet him in doute.
þerfore Crist for oure foliȝe
Was beten with skurgis al aboute.

Inficit et gustum gula sensum dans
ebetatum,   Contra gulam
Set reddit iustum os iusti felle potatum.
Glotonie schent oure tast
And dulle makt oure wittes alle.
But remedie þerto þu hast
Of Crist þat drank þe bitter galle.

dex 197.   Clauduntur, st. 3] Claduntur MS.

58

ibid.

219.   f. 131   Modo:

Gula is samel[es];

Luxuria is laweles;

Ira is rithfulness;

Inuidia is holiness

Accidia is feblesse;

Superbia in pris;

Cupiditas is holden wys.

Margin damaged; l. 1 at least has lost some letters. Cf. Index and Suppl.
1791.

De Religione

220.   f. 134   Nota quod si religiosus esse volueris quod stringaris vinculis.
Oportet:

þe foot of þi wil be bounde in þe bond of chastete;

þe hond of þi werk be bounde in þe bond of charite;

þat þin heued of þi strengþe be bounde in þe bond of obedienc

And þe nekke of þin owen wil be bounde in þe bond of pacienc

Oportet enim quod:

Pedes tue affeccionis stringantur vinculo castitatis

De Resurexione

221.   f. 135^V Nota quod resurexio Christi fuit multipliciter, in signum
qualis debet esse resurrexio peccatoris a culpa. Nam Christus
resurexit, ita homo vere:

Vere per detestacionem peccatorum

f. 136   Sothliche with trewe sennes forsakingge;

Erliche with hastif penance takingge;

Priueliche þoru bedes of gode frendis;

Dredfuliche with open withstonding to þe fendes;

Worchifuliche with gode werkes doyngge;

Openliche with good ensample in beringge;

Stedefastliche with[outen] ony aȝen-fallingge.

The seven English lines all have Latin equivalents on f. 135^V. withouten,
l. 7] with MS (Latin: Et permanenter et per finalem perseueranciam).

59

De Reddenda Racione

222.   f. 140^v   Oportet te reddere racionem:

Of þe graces þat God hat þe sent,

Of þe godis þat God hat þe lent,

And of þi time, hou it is ispent.

De Superbia

223.   f. 143^v   [3]ef þu be riche and wys in lore,

In tunge gracious,

[Pri]de destruiȝet þis an more,

For he is venimous.

Si tibi copia, si sapientia formaque detur

Initia 17998, Sprichw. 29238.   3ef, Pride] ef, de MS (ms. damaged).

Pride: superbia (l. 2 of Latin).

ibid.

224.   f. 144   It is nouth worth to a child his frendis g[oodnesse]

But if his owen gode þewe reule is herte with r[it];

Often he begyt here is bred þat hadde is fader kn[it];

Efsones is he gret lord þat first was pore in s[othnesse].

Nihil prodest filio probitas parentis

Nisi virtus propria dominetur mentis;

Mendicat multociens filius potentis;

Regnat e contrario natus indigentis.

Index 1636 (includes no. 225 below). Ms. damage to the end of all four

English lines.   frendis: for another example of frend = parens see MED

s.v. frend n. 4 (a 1387).   sothnesse: the conjecture is not offered with

confidence.   For another occurrence of the Latin see N. Davis Review of

English Studies   NS XX   (1969) 48.

ibid.

225.   f. 144   þenk of þi cote þat is brith an gay,

Hou it sal ben lined with grene and with gr[ey].

Suppl. 3567.6. grey] gr MS (margin damaged).   The presumed warning

in the tag 'green and grey' (see MED s.v. grene n.(1), (c)) is obscure.

60

ibid.

226.   f. 144^v   Wat heylet man? Qui is he prud?

Wat ned hat he of riche scrud?

In lust of senne he is wrouth,

In harde peines hider brouth.

Wo and traualie is is liuing,

Nedi and naked in his dey3ing.

þou he be fair and strong in fith

To wirmes mete he sal ben dith.

His faire eyne in þe heued sul senke,

His gay bodi foul sal stinke.

þus solen we turnen, child an man,

In puder of herde an be no man.

<u>Index</u> 3903.

ibid.

227.   f. 146   Gret heynesse of blod,

Richesse and wele of good,

Of bodi and soule mith,

Mani man makt prud in is owen sith.

Nobilitas generis, prelacio copia rerum

<u>Initia</u> 11859, <u>Sprichw</u>. 17017.

ibid.

228.   f. 146^v   Behold nou, man, quat þu salt be,

þat al þis werd nou drawith to þe.

A foul caroni3e on þe to se

þat schinest nou so fair in ble.

Vide, qualis eris, [qui] mundi gaudia queris.

<u>Sprichw</u>. 33309f; two lines in Grimestone.   qui] om. MS (<u>ms. damaged</u>).

De Sapientia

229. f. 151ᵛ   ʒif þu wis worþe wel,

þese sex kep wich i þe kenne:

Wat þu seyst, wam til,

Of wąm, and wy, wer, an wanne.

Si sapiens fore vis, sex serua, que tibi mando:

Quid vel vbi loqueris, de quo, cui, quomodo, quando.

Suppl. 1436.5 (but not noted in this manuscript).   Initia 17963,
Sprichw. 29127.   Whiting, S75 (not noted here).

ibid.

230. f. 151ᵛ   He is wis þat can ben war or he is wo;

He is wis þat louet is frend and is fo;

He is wis þat hat inou and þanne seit 'Ho';

He is wis þat dotʒ ay wel an seit ay so.

Index and Suppl. 1139.   Whiting, W45 (not noted here).

ibid.

231. f. 151ᵛ   Kunne to speke worchipe is; worchipe is cunne be stille;

[þ]is to ʒif þu cunne mith, no word ne saltu neuere spille.

Scire loqui decus est, decus est et scire tacere:

Hec duo si poteris scire, peritus eris.

Sprichw. 27621.   þis] is MS (ms. damaged).

De Sanctitate

232. f. 152   Secundum Remigium, Sanctitas depingitur ad similitudinem

virginis, faciem habent[is] auersam mundo. In cuius circuitu

depingebantur 3 circuli: in 1° circulo scribebatur 'Amor'

et in circuitu iste versus; in 2° circulo 'Hono[r]' et in

circuitu iste versus; in 3° circul[o] 'Timor' et in circuitu

iste versus:

ʒef þu sekest loue and wilt him finde,

In holinesse þi lif þu binde.

ʒef þu wilt han worchipe þat may neuere slake,

Holinesse fast hold, and senne þu forsake.

ʒef þu wilt ben dred and men to þe luten,

Holinesse euere hold withinnen and eek withouten.

Index 1432. The picture has not been traced in Remigius. The three couplets are connected by red lines to the three captions of the introduction; no Latin verses are given in the ms. habentis, Honor, circulo (iii)] habent, Hono, circul MS (ms. damaged).

De Tempore

233. f. 154 Ecce nunc tempus:

For to criȝen to God for helpe in al oure nedes;

For to aspiȝen þis werd, oure fles, þe deueles redes;

For to tellen oure scrif-fader al oure misdedes;

And for to sellen bodily godes in elmes dedes.

II Corinthians vi 2 (Latin only).

ibid.

234. f. 154 þu faire fles þat art me dere,

Nou art þu fo, nou artu fere.

Wan I þe fede as king of lond,

I lese my time, I ere þe sond.

O quam cara caro, rationi consona raro

ibid.

235. f. 154ᵛ For lore of godes I wepe sore,

But more for lore of day.

þou godes ben lorn, I may han more;

Time lorn aȝen comen ne may.

Dampna fleo rerum, set plus fleo dampna dierum

Index 829 (not 'one quatrain and four couplets'). Initia 4042, Sprichw. 4893.

ibid.

236. f. 154ᵛ Bisiliche ȝef þe to lore

See above, f. 98, no.140.

ibid.

237.   f. 154^v   Hou sort a feste it is, þe ioyȝe of al þis werd,

Als þe schadwe is of man in þis midel-herd,

þat oftentime withdrawith þe blisse withouten ende,

And driuet man to helle to ben `þer´ with þe fende.

Quam breue festum est hec mundi gaudia

Index 1262.   Whiting W671 (this ex. not noted);   cf. here nos.   19, 83,
and 103.

ibid.

238.   f. 154^v   Wil time is of forȝeuing

Amend þe of þi wikke leuing.

For afterward þe time sal come

þat forȝefnesse sal ben þe benome.

Peniteant miseri dum tempus sit miserendi

Index 4084.

De Tribulacione

239.   f. 154^v   [...]e I þenke of wordis þre

[...]ay myn herte be:

[...]n is þat I sal awey;

[...]þer is I ne wot wat day;

þe þridde is my moste care,

þat I ne wot wider to fare.

Index and Suppl. 3969.   Ms. damaged.   For Latin versions and analogues
(there are none here) see EL XIII, pp. 172-3, and Woolf, p. 86.

De Temptacione

240.   f. 157^v   Periculosissima temptacio est nulla temptacione pulsari,

quia qui non temptatur quatuor mala incurrit que

sunt:

Pride of herte and hey beringge;

Of þi time euel spendingge;

Of oþer[es] dedis misdemingge,

And of is owen vnkunningȝe.

Cordis eleuacio, mentis et corporis vagacio

Attributed in the ms. to Augustine.   oþeres] oþereres MS.

64

De Voluntate

241. f. 158^V [...] wil is good wel for to do

[...]t quan my liking comet, good wil is go.

[...] mihi adiacet perficere, autem non inuenio.

Ms. damaged.

De Veritate

242. f. 162   Veritas habet:

Fewe hereres,

Feynte wereres,

Manie bacbiteres,

And dredful spekeres.

Paucos auditores

De Via Christi

243. f. 166^V Al þe wey þat God goth by

[I]s sothfastnesse and mercy.

Omnes vie Domini tue misericordia et veritas.

Tobias iii 2.   Is] s MS (ms. damaged).

ibid.

244. f. 166^V Nota quod via Christi vel vita fuit:

[...]nesse an buxumnesse;

[...]uerte and sarpnesse;

[...]nesse and hardnesse.

Ms. damaged.

ibid.

[þu:]

245. f. 166^V [...]alt dreden God for he wrouthte þe;

Salt louen God for he bouthte þe;

[...]alt trosten in God for he fedit þe;

Salt folwen God for he ledit þe.

Ms. damaged.

ibid.

246.   f. 166^v   Venit:

With fles al bespred,

With blod al bebled,

þe wikke for to demen

And þe gode for to ȝemen.

66

First Line Index of English Verse

Varieties of spelling are ignored in the arrangement, and for convenience of reference the spelling norm is that of modern English. The first line is always indexed under the first English word (e.g. no. 17 is entered under Maket not Pecunia, no. 100 under Is not Luxuria; similarly, no. 88 is entered under þoru not Diabolus, and no. 219 under Is not Gula). The number following the line is the Descriptive Index number.

A Iesu so fair an fre, 210.

A Iesu, þin holi heued, 200.

A barge to beren fro depe groundes, 51.

A fals beginningge, 46.

A fals tresorer, see To a fals ... (no. 142).

A filthe þat God almithten hateȝ, 145.

A scheld of red, a cros of grene, 182.

A sory beuerech it is and sore it is abouth, 174.

After þat þe appel was eten withouten detȝ passed non of alle, 144.

Aȝen my felawes þat I haue spoken, 59.

Allas, allas, þis werdis blisse lestet but a stounde, 103.

Allas for sennes þat I haue wrouth, 148.

Allas, Iesu, þi loue is lorn, 168.

Allas, wo sal myn herte slaken, 187.

Al mi blod for þe is sched, 170.

Al oure wele and al oure lif, 218.

Al þe wey þat God goth by, 243.

Alle þe wordis þat drawen to senne, 11.

Alle we liuen hapfuliche, 124.

Als a clerk withnesset of wisdom þat can, 102.

Als a se flouwende, 84.

Als I lay vpon a nith / Alone in my longging, 5.

Als I lay vpon a nith / I lokede vpon a stronde, 7.

At Domesday we solen vprise, 198a.

At þe time of matines, Lord, þu were itake, 4.

Bare was þat quite brest, 179 (cf. no. 154).

Be lou and louende, 86.

Be þe wel, be þe wo, be þeself mynde, 91.

Ber þe wel an quemfuliche, 80.

Behold, man, wat is my wo, 204.

Behold nou, man, quat þu salt be, 228.

Behold þe þornes myn heued han þrongen -- hou sarpe þat it ben, 206.

Behold þu, man, her myth þu se, 195.

Behold, þu wreche, withouten strif, 216.

Behold, womman, a dolful sith, 181.

Betre is þe pore in his si[m]plesse, 70.

Be war, man, I come as þef, 110.

Blissed ben men pore with wil, 38.

Blissed moten þo pappes be, 36.

Bisiliche ȝef þe to lore, 140, 236.

But I me bethouthte, 189.

Charite is brithe of word, 47.

Children ben litel, brith and schene, and eþe for to fillen, 50.

Crist criȝede wan he preyȝede forȝefnesse of oure senne, 162.

Crist is offred for mannis sake, 188.

Crist lay an loude gredde, 171.

Cristis blod, þe heyȝe of lif, þre þinggis it hat vndon, 190.

Cristis bodi maltȝ, 163.

Clernesse of vnderstondingge, 32.

Comet, ȝe children, me for to heren, 72.

Deth is a dredful dettour, 112.

Deth is lif, 132.

Drau þe neuere to man, 108.

Dred and loue, hate an good, 79.

Drunkenchipe brekt, 77.

Herde maket halle, 130.

Eyne to seing, 137.

Fewe hereres, 242.

Fle þe dich of senne, 143.

For I ham pore, withouten frendes, 129.

For lore of godes I wepe sore, 235.

For þat appel þat Eue tok, 146.

For þing þat is to askyn, 2.

For to criȝen to God for helpe in al oure nedes, 233.

Frenchipe is felounie, 26.

ȝef þi godis wil it ben þine, 68.

God ouer alle þingge, 87.

Gold and al þis werdis wyn, 203.

God Lord þat sittes in trone, 176.

Gret heynesse of blod, 227.

Heil Marie, an wel þe be, 33.

Hand, heued, foot, herte, 159.

Harde gates I haue go, 164.

Haue detȝ in mende, 119.

Haue o god in worchipe, 217.

He is wis þat can ben war or he is wo, 230.

He makt himself in gret richesse, 43.

He taket oþer coloures arith, 48.

He þat alle þing doth wel, 35.

He þat is king of alle londis, 55.

He þat louet his frend and fo, 28, 64.

He þat time borwith fro morwe to morwen, 114.

He þat was al heuene with him þat al hat wrouth, 166.

Hem þat ben naked ȝif cloþing, 105.

Her sal I duellen, loken vnder ston, 128.

His colour blaket, 127.

Hold forwarde and be stedefast, see þat I, wrecche ... (no. 49).

Hou hard it was, and wat distresse, 156.

Hou sort a feste it is, þe ioyȝe of al þis werd, 237.

Of þe graces þat God hat þe sent, 222.

On mo[r]ewe morwen comet al oure care, 117.

On þe tre he hatȝ iborn, 24.

Oure fader, þat art in heuene onon, 135.

Oure peynes ben grille and felle, 93.

Pes be, 150.

Pore and hungri þat han nede, 37.

Pride of herte and hey beringge, 240.

Rediliche, withouten abiding, 212.

Riche and pore, ȝung and old, 120.

Rith as man may se, 198.

Reuthe made God on mayden to lithte, 167 (cf. no. 25).

Sey nou, man, quat þinkest þu, 126.

Sey, þu vessel of wrechidnesse, 122.

Seth faste þi fot on rode-tre, 157.

[S]alt dreden God for he wrouthte þe, 245.

Sort arn mennis dayȝes; his monis ben told also, 109.

Siker is det to alle maner men, 125.

Senful man, beþing and se, 202.

Senful man, ne dred þe nouth, 40.

Softeliche senne gennet in wende, 101.

Sothliche with trewe sennes forsakingge, 221.

Sorfulhed of detȝ þat stant an waitet þe, 138.

Spere and cros, nail, detȝ and þorn, 158.

Suich semblant Crist sal maken to þe aboue, 76.

Suete sone, reu on me, and brest out of þi bondis, 178.

Tel nouth þin frend al þat [. . .], 3.

þat fastingge withouten elmesse is of mith, 95.

þat I, wrecche, þat senful was, 49.

þe day taket his lith, 82.

þe flour springende, see To þe flour . . . (no. 73).

þe foot of þi wil be bounde in þe bond of chastete, 220.

þe garlond þat of þorn is wroth, 199.

þe ȝefte faliȝet nouth with skil, 74, 75 (þe ȝifte of hand faliȝet . . .).

þe pore man oueral litȝ stille, 153.

þe rede stremes renning, 191.

þe schip in þe seyling, 151.

þe slauwe man is but a driȝe tre þat no froit wil beren, 21.

þe þing þat þu mauth lesen, clep et nouth þin owen, 18.

þe wise herte and vnderstondingge, 12.

þe werd with is faired, 131.

þe þanne, we beseken, þi seruans do good, 134.

þanne is abstinence of worþinesse, 13.

þer as al þe herte of man, see þus is al ... (no. 161).

þei ben nouth wel for to leuen, 14, 61.

þei þat ben trewe in louingge, 66.

þin herte with spere stiked, 197.

þenk, man, þi loue was dere ibouth, 207.

þenk of þi cote þat is brith an gay, 225.

þis is my bodi als ȝe mov se, 56.

þu faire fles þat art me dere, 234.

þu man, þat wilt knowen þiself, loke quat þu hast þouth, 41.

[þu slalt dreden God for he wrouthte þe, see [S]alt dreden ... (no. 245).

þu schendest me sore with þi loking, 141.

þu sikest sore, 201.

þu þat hangest þer so heyȝe, 183.

þoru pride of herte and heynesse, 88.

þoru suetnesse of lore in preching, 71.

þus is al þe herte of man, 161.

To a fals tresorer, 142.

To eueri preysing is knit a knot, 58.

To pleyȝen and ragen is for þi pru, 20.

To sorwe and to care turned is my pley (no. 92), see Into sorwe ... (no. 39).

To þe flour springende, 73.

To waxen riche with gret blame, 42.

Trewe withouten quey[n]tise and feiningge, 65.

Vndo þi dore, my spuse dere, 186.

Vpon þe rode I am for þe, 209.

Water and blod for þe I suete, 214.

We ben heled þat eer wer seke, 160.

Wat heylet man?   Qui is he prud, 226.

Wat is more dred, 10.

Watso þu art þat gost her be me, 115.

[Wann]e I þenke of wordis þre, 239.

Wanne þe sunne rist, see þe day taket ... (no. 82).

Wan þu makst ingong, 152.

Quil men and wemmen woniȝen togidere, 97.

Wil þu art in welthe and wele, 89.

Wil time is of forȝeuing, 238.

With it was his naked brest, and red is blodi side, 154 (cf. no. 179).

Wo þe þus beseþ, Iesu, my suete lif, 165.

Woso louet nouth to don orith, 149.

Woso þouthte of his birthe, 139.

Woso wile ben riche and hauing, 69.

Woso wile in soule hauen blisse, 44.

Wy haue ȝe no reuthe on my child, 34.

With a sorwe and a clut, 116.

With fles al bespred, 246.

Wordes ben so knit with sinne, 63.

Werdis blisse maket me blind, 19.

Werdis ioyȝe is menkt with wo, 83.

Ȝe suln turnen to God, see Rediliche ... (no. 212).

Ȝe þat pasen be þe weyȝe, 211.

Ȝe þat wilen heuene winne, 98.

Ȝungþe ne can nouth but leden me wil, 52.

Imperfect First Lines

The following first lines, damaged in the manuscript, cannot be reconstructed with certainty:

[. . .] wil is good wel for to do, 241.

[. . .]nesse an buxumnesse, 244.

Printed in June 2019
by Rotomail Italia S.p.A., Vignate (MI) - Italy